Interlude:
Letters from a
Foreign Correspondent

Interlude:
Letters from a
Foreign Correspondent

Mary Archer St. Clair
with
Mollie H. Washburne

BRANDYLANE PUBLISHERS
White Stone, Virginia

❋ Brandylane Publishers

P.O. Box 261, White Stone, Virginia 22578
(804) 435-6900 or 1 800 553-6922; e-mail: brandy@crosslink.net

Library of Congress Cataloging-in-Publication Data

St. Clair, Mary Archer, 1906–
      Interlude: letters from a foreign correspondent/Mary Arhcer St. Clair.
            p.   cm.
      ISBN 1-883911-21-4
      1. Greene, Roger Denise—Correspondence. 2. Foreign
correspondents—United States—Correspondence. 3. St. Clair, Mary
Archer, 1906–   Correspondence. I. Title.
PN4874.G684S8 1997
070.4′332′092—dc21
  [B]   97-32022
                                    CIP

In memory of
Roger D. Greene
and
F. Scott Fitzgerald

Prologue

When I returned from my Grand Tour of Europe that spring, there was a letter from him. It was tucked in a pile of mail my parents had stacked on my dressing table. His letter I kept, not because I was madly in love with him or because I thought I would be one day. I just could not throw it away. I saved the next letter from him, too, and the next. I have them all.

Almost seventy years later, I open the first letter again. I read it slowly. There is no rush these days. I used to race through his letters, eager to get to the next word, phrase, paragraph. Now I look upon them with the gift of remembrance.

The letters have been with me through many moves. Today, I am packing them up once more to go with me to an apartment in a retirement community. My daughter cannot believe I have all these letters and that they are in such good shape. She does not know that she is a part of some of them. I think I should tell her, but first I must get moved and settled.

I glance through some of the other letters and put them in the box. There is still a disposition to his writing that attracts me. It is witty, dramatic, moving, and shy. It is my friend Roger Greene. I saw him only twice, but for a while we had a friendship so personal and improbable that it seemed almost invented.

Jan. 12, 1925
347-24th St.
Santa Monica

Mary Lou dearest—

I don't like that opening—it is awfully weak and doesn't tell half enough. So you see I'm in a very sentimental mood tonight and would probably breath amorous madrigals in your delightful ears were you present. As it is I can only feel as sad as a sixteen year old boy over his first love affair—and . . . that is awfully sad—tragic.

Gods! Mary Lou, your letter was just damnably sweet and although I know you don't mean half what you've written, it strikes a hidden chord that makes me want to say a lot of silly (yet true) things. I always thought my vocabulary was rather prolific—but I find that when I want to tell you just how damn much you mean to me—it is pitifully weak and limited!

Gods! are you going to be gone until the first of April? That is going to put an awful dent in me if you are because somehow Bluefield isn't too far away, but when you start cruising around Europe—that will be terrible. And then, while we may never see each other again or at least for some time, I am horribly jealous, and the thought of M.L. gazing with some dashing Lothario at a pale, Mediterranean moon—well, it causes more than a bit of anguish.

All of which summed up—if you see what I mean—is that Mary Lou is far and away the loveliest and sweetest girl on four continents.

O! lady, you shouldn't tell me you like me a little because it only makes it worse. You don't mind my moaning on like this, do you? I said I was in a bad mood tonight—but you are going so far and I know you'll never find time to write.

Ha! It is so damn pleasant to be sad. I've almost decided I'm the saddest and most melancholy man in the world—that you are the most adorable and unattainable, like some ethereal goddess, so that somehow I feel incomparably happy and forlorn.

I promised that some day I would burst into poetry for you. I find I am no poet—my metre somehow won't work right and it is a beastly job to try to say in rime what I mean in prose. However:

Like some skylark up on high
I seem to hear her far off cry
That rends and wounds my senses till
Her message comes to leave its thrill
of future joys and sorrow.

And so I wait in saddened mood
And dream of love in solitude
I wonder what the storm clouds mean—
What wrath of gods, what angry spleen
Will hold her song the morrow?

Ah! life is just a world of sighs
Of anguished looks and tearful eyes
Where men and women play at love
Like puppets ruled by Him above
and passion throbs in gloomy den

And so I wait in saddened mood
And dream of love in solitude
Yet hoping patiently and still,
For what seems centuries until
Her song comes once again.

Isn't that frightful? But I feel better after uncaging all that.
Thank God I never wanted to be a poet. It would be ghastly. I
would eat my heart out in a fortnight if I had to turn out things
like that. Poetry is just a mood—you go into a state of coma and
everything psychic comes out in black and white . . . every mood
or passion.

Well, Mary Lou, please write me very often. And now, before
I start wondering how maddeningly alluring your lips look when
you smile, I must drop the curtain and extinguish the midnight
oil. When the mystic hour strikes and the graveyard watch begins,
I become too romantic, imaginative (and childish, I suppose) for
this materialistic world. Good bye—bon voyage—and oh! Mary
Lou—just an awful lot of love.

from
Roge

3

Chapter 1

I boarded the train for Princeton on a glorious spring day in 1924. Redbuds and dogwoods decorated the countryside with their elfin blooms, "fulfilling the promise of the season," I wrote in my journal. But even an overcast day would not have dampened my excitement and curiosity about going to the Freshman Prom with a blind date.

His name was Roger Greene. He was from California, but had come east to attend Andover before entering Princeton University. He was almost twenty. He was smart and interesting and wanted to be a writer. His suitemate knew I would like him.

Gordon McNeer had arranged the date and supplied me with the information about Roge, pronounced "Raj," he told me. My acceptance of the proposal required little persuasion from Gordon. A trip to Princeton, a prom, and a mystery boy from California were a winning combination.

Gordon thought I would be keen about the idea because he knew me well. He and my brother, Frank, were both at Princeton, though Frank was in his senior year and Gordon was a freshman. Prior to Princeton, Gordon spent many holidays and vacations at our home because his family was too far away in Alaska. He was bright and delightful, and I liked him all the more because he did not treat me like the kid sister of his good friend. Unlike my brother, he recognized that I was grown up, sophisticated, and a worthwhile companion; I was seventeen.

I had just graduated from the Oakhurst Collegiate School, an all-girl, boarding school above the Ohio River in Cincinnati. My world had been widened by my education there. I was proficient in French and knew some Italian and had been tremendously influenced by my study of history, art, and architecture.

I hoped to pursue a degree in art history and fancied myself a painter or artist of some sort. College could have been the next step, but I had been bitten by the European bug, as had many of my contemporaries. The war was over, the exchange rate was good, and Europe was the place to be.

So, it was with a triumphant sigh that I returned to my home in Bluefield, West Virginia, a coal-inspired town on the southwest Virginia border. My parents were proud of my accomplishments at Oakhurst. They valued education and believed knowledge made us appreciative of the world around us and gave us respect for all cultures. I wanted to experience that appreciation first-hand and asked for a trip to Europe.

My parents agreed, knowing that such trips were well-chaperoned and advisable for young women. It was a glamorous thing to do after boarding school when the avenue to college was not paved with similar incentives for women.

When Gordon phoned about the Princeton weekend, I was still in the planning stages of my Grand Tour of Europe. My parents decided to coincide a trip to New York for a long weekend and allowed me to take the train from the city to Princeton Junction.

Gordon, Roge, and another friend were waiting at the station when I arrived shortly after noon. Gordon greeted me with hugs and a kiss and an introduction to a tall, handsome young man with a well-built, athletic figure.

"Roge, this is Mary Lou that I've told you so much about!"

Roge stammered a hello and not much more. It seems Gordon had informed Roge that I was a real live Southern belle. Roge, having never come face to face with a daughter of Dixieland, was speechless. He was very polite, and there was a sweetness and honesty about him that was apparent. I was sure I would like him.

We piled into a borrowed car, a Chrysler two-seater with a rumble seat, and roared off to the inn. The other girls were there already, including Gordon's date whom I knew well. After quick introductions and a comb through the hair, we drove over to Roge and Gordon's suite where their roommates were waiting for us to have tea. British habits were very popular then.

All the while, I kept a casual eye on Roge and he on me. He was well-mannered and attentive, but very quiet. His eyes, I remember, had a curious look about them. I was anxious to talk to him alone, away from the banter.

The prom was a lovely affair. Upon arriving, Roge's first duty was to find the chaperone line and take me over for introductions. We went down the line saying hello and giving my name in a very proper style. It was not an unpleasant obligation, but one that Roge and I performed with dispatch and mutual amusement.

Roge was a good dancer, not flashy, but not uncertain about it either. He never seemed to take his eyes off me, and I wondered what I looked like to him. I believed myself to be too practical and athletic to be truly pretty, and I was tall at 5 feet, 8 inches. But, I thought Roge's gaze was complimentary.

We shifted from dancing to talking. He was so different from the drawling Southern boys I knew, always quick with a line and oozing all that charm. He was charming in a quiet way that I found appealing. His thoughts and questions were earnest and personal. I responded directly, and I think my serious, studious side surprised him since he believed Southern girls were given to swooning and syrupy talk.

I felt comfortable with him and we talked a lot, sharing ideas and observations and finding we had a common ground despite our dissimilar backgrounds. We were young and eager and interested in everything, and felt older than our years. We both wanted to travel. We believed our thoughts were cosmopolitan, open-minded, jazzy. We were unabashedly definite about our goals; we were very young.

Roge wanted to write more than anything. With F. Scott

Fitzgerald in mind, he wanted to chronicle our generation. I remember talking about Fitzgerald that night as we walked around the university. We even paid a visit to Fitzgerald's old eating club—Cottage—where my brother Frank was engaged in nocturnal musings with fellow members. Fitzgerald had recently written that his generation had "grown up to find all gods dead, all wars fought, all faiths in man shaken." Roge more or less agreed with this philosophy, but I did not, and we continued walking on the heels of Fitzgerald's "Lost Generation."

Roge was the youngest of three boys. His mother was a great beauty, he said. I seem to remember that he said she wanted to be an actress or had been, but I could be wrong about that. He said nothing about his father that I can recall. One brother was also at Princeton, the other at Yale, and all had attended Andover. Roge had been born in Cleveland, Ohio, but they had moved often. Santa Monica was their latest home address.

Wanderlust was something we both had in common, especially that night. By dawn we were still wandering and talking. We met up with friends who had cars and drove around the country roads. Prohibition was the law, but I did not drink much, and ended up behind the wheel. I considered driving just as thrilling as a nip from the bootleg bottle.

Near Princeton Junction, we stopped a dairy truck just beginning its rounds and sipped early morning milk while watching the pink dawning of a new day. Roge had thoughts about a novel that would include me. We planned to meet in New York later that day.

After a bit of sleep back at the inn, I took the train with the rest of the college crowd going into New York for the weekend. My parents were staying at the Biltmore and were waiting for me. That afternoon I met Roge under the legendary clock where all the young people assembled.

We went with a crowd to a favorite Chinese restaurant on the west side and then over to a dance "palace" where a huge band was playing. Roge and the other boys bought dance tickets after we found a table. When we wanted to dance, we gave our ticket to an usher who let us through a gate onto a huge dance floor. It was loads of fun.

There was a speakeasy in the Brownstone district where the

Princeton crowd was well-known. It was on a good side street and had the appearance of a home. The owner inspected us through a peep hole in the large door before letting us in.

Inside, we went upstairs to a lovely small restaurant and bar. The establishment was run by Italians, who were gracious to us. The favorite drink was an Alexander cocktail—gin, creme de cacao, and cream. I had one, and it tasted divine.

Roge and I said good-bye that evening, optimistic about each other and our own dreams. Of course, back then every meeting held the potential for something grand. Such young and happy days, a beautiful and carefree time of life. We promised to write each other during the summer and meet again in the fall when he returned to Princeton.

Though our meeting seemed a passing thing, a great feeling had developed between us, a feeling that went deeper than either of us realized at the time. We had only just met, and yet we had a history. It was a personal experience that touched upon something larger, but even Roge could not then express the meaning of it in words.

Chapter 2

The following January, I sailed from New York aboard the S.S. *Lapland* on my first Atlantic crossing. For more than four months, I traveled with a small group of girls chaperoned by a retired dean of Hollins College.

Before leaving the Hotel Collingwood in New York, I sent Roge a letter full of excitement and my itinerary. We had not kept our promise to write each other. Both of us were too busy and young to honor such a vow. But I decided to let him know my plans to travel were underway.

That wonderful journey through Europe and the Middle East flickers through my mind now like a silent movie. I see the monkeys chattering on the rocks at Gibraltar, the casinos of Monte Carlo, the black statue of Madonna and child in Algeria. I am standing in the Acropolis and then sipping thick, Turkish coffee in the Old Bazaar of Constantinople. I am at the impossibly British Allenby Hotel in Jerusalem, home base for our tour of the Holy Land. Then, I hear the Muslim chants in Cairo, and I am riding a camel to see the pyramids and Sphinx at Giza. The sun sinks into the Nile, and I veil my face to ward off the flies on a carriage ride to the ruins at Luxor, where I descend into the recently discovered tomb of the boy pharaoh, Tutankhamen.

All those images were on my mind when I returned to West

Virginia and found Roge's letter on my dressing table. I was glad he had responded and amused by his poetry. I wondered about him, but I also wondered about Harry Manning, the stunning young sea captain I had met returning aboard the S.S. *America*.

I was glad to be home among familiar sights and sounds, but more than eager to go back. I wrote to Roge and happily received another letter from him.

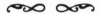

Aug. 20, 1925
316 - 25th St.
Santa Monica, California

Mary Lou—

O! it was good to hear from you once more, see your handwriting again and madly believe that you had not utterly forgotten me.

Your postal—and a vision of Mary Lou—came like a white, white star where there was only blue before.

You know—I had quite lost you . . . that trip to exotic lands and then I lost the list of your port of calls and you seemed so very far away—half the earth stood between us and even now it is a long time between mails from Bluefield to Santa Monica.

But I had not forgotten Mary Lou—that, if you will believe me, is forever impossible.

I have so much to tell and ask you—it is difficult to begin. What I really need is about an hour's tea date with you at the Biltmore or Plaza or that funny Chinese place we went—or anywhere, just so I could talk and listen to you.

God only knows when that will be, though, for unless a miracle takes place Princeton's portals will not harbor R. Denise this year. I am starting an agitation in the family now to trek to New York late in the fall, and although nothing intelligent has been said either way, I hope and believe it may pan out. If so, you will just have to come up and teach me the Charleston. Out west here everybody raves so much about the Charleston that I feel rather dignified in saying coldly—"No, I don't dance the Charleston."

With you it would be different. Indeed I could do a cake walk with Mary Lou.

Had a letter yesterday from Johnny Moss—remember him? A very lugubrious letter in which he accused me of backsliding on coming back to Princeton and solemnly asserted something I told him long ago, "Southern girls are the only kind." I mean to write him about that "s" on girls.

Still pounding out copy on the Santa Monica Outlook newspaper—sports editor. This and next week I'm on vacation and it is glorious. Eighteen holes of golf in the morning—a swim in the Pacific—eighteen more holes and then I write for the rest of the afternoon and evening. Doing a short story, my first serious attempt.

If it is published and you should see it, I am discovered—for the lovely lady in it is Mary Lou. God! a creature "the tender arch of her scarlet lips, the gentle mysticism of her eyes, infinitely blue, the subtle fragrance of her golden hair . . ."

Always,
Roger

I was surprised to learn that Roger Denise Greene was not going back to Princeton after all. (Denise was a middle name that caused Roge some anguish.) I did not know if it was a money matter or just his need to be caught up in the traffic of the world rather than academic life. I really did not know many particulars about his family.

Education and travel had become one in the same to me, but I was unable to stage a return to Europe. The next plan, which my parents endorsed, was to attend Holton Arms Junior College, a two year college for women in Washington, D.C. It was more than a finishing school, but less rigorous than a regular college.

After a few weeks of classes, Mrs. Holton took a particular interest in me and decided to direct my studies in art history. She felt I was "college material" and urged me to consider going to college where she felt I belonged. I thought about her advice, but my desire to be on the other side of the Atlantic was very strong.

I let Roge know I was turning over a new leaf and settling

back into school. If only he had returned to Princeton, we could have gotten together. In person, I was sure I could have supplied him with more details for that "lovely lady" in his novel.

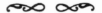

September 18, 1925

Mary Lou—

There is no need of an adjective—to say dearest Mary Lou would be but repetition; for in all the world there is only one Mary Lou . . .

Your very wonderful letter came today and—do you think me temperamental?—I confess to an odd sensation of melancholia somewhat exotically mixed with brimming happiness.

To hear the sixth century poet of China in "The Lute of Jade":—

High o'er the hill the moon barque steers.
The lantern lights depart.
Dead springs are stirring in my heart;
And there are tears . . .
But that which makes my grief more deep
Is that you know not when I weep.

Rather beautiful, isn't it? I am certainly with you about turning over a new leaf, for while I cannot see you, there comes something like a stiletto-thrust thrill to read your letters and just imagine that Mary Lou's voice is singing like the throaty call of a nightingale raising up its evensong . . .

So—here I sit at my desk trying futilely to conjure up words to tell you—ah! what? It is there one moment and the next is lost in a maze of meaningless letters and stark, cold words that mean nothing.

It is very fine, your going back to school and—since jealousy is a primeval instinct—I confess to a fierce joy that you will probably not see any dashing genus homo long enough to fall desperately in love.

About my story—I've let it get "cold" for the past two or three weeks and on re-reading it discover the usual amount of things that need patching—things that were overlooked in the fierce heat of composition.

I wrote it during my week's vacation, but being "on the ball" again, I find little time to retouch it . . . which is just an excuse for saying that I am too frightfully lazy and would rather read the latest novel. Just finished A. Hamilton Gibbs' "Soundings"—a delightful story which left me wondering if I can ever turn out anything as good.

I've been playing heaps of golf. I'm just three blocks from a beautiful course and every afternoon finds me playing 18 holes. You see, I work—or play at work—from shortly before 8 o'clock till 2:30 or 3:30 and then slip away. Made a 39 on the first nine holes the other day, but I blush to say what the second nine was like.

I always thought of California, somehow, as the land of mañana—a sleepy place where one lay in hammocks and downed "mint juleps" and watched the sun-kist oranges become sun-kist.

Unfortunately, it is quite the reverse. One dashes hither and yon quite madly doing all sorts of things. I have little time to read anymore, but have sworn a great and solemn oath to become a recluse in the near future.

I would give my last three dollars to return to Princeton this fall—but, alack!—three dollars falls a bit below the mark.

Guess you will be stepping to all the proms this winter. If you go to New Haven, be sure and look up my brother, Frank. He's a senior this year, captain of the 150 lb. varsity crew, and would love to meet you—since I've told him all about you until he threw books at me. And in spite of the fact that I've known you so very little, I didn't need to improvise.

Ye gods! It does seem odd how little we've been together. In New York, when you thought I was a little drunk—but I can swear it was only at the sight of Mary Lou—and those swift-passing moments at Princeton when everything moved hazily—I seemed in a murky fog—and Mary Lou was gone before I had quite realized that the poignant joy of seeing you again had come and departed.

15

I'm playing in another Theater Guild production—Zoe Akins' "Daddy's Gone A-Hunting." Rather a melodramatic piece in which the heroine's voice goes tremolo half the time and loses all control the other half. If there's a dry handkerchief left in the audience after the show, it will only be because the moronic intelligentsia of the fair city thinks it is high comedy.

Everybody is going back to college now. It hurts a little not to be with them, but the terrible, terrible thing is to have high school boys call me "Mr. Greene" when I go over there for a story or have to sit on the speakers' platform on Washington's birthday or some similar occasion. If anybody tells me my hair is retreating I shall go to Paris, drink the dregs—and plunge into the Seine—which, I am told, is the proper exit for young men of dubious genius.

And so to bed to read Michael Arlen's "Mayfair." As the closing line of my story goes: "O! my dear, didn't you know that I—that I loved you—long ago?"

Roger

⚬⚬ ⚬⚬

Roge was a boost. His letters were unlike the others I received, and I kept saving them. I wrote to him about the museums, my studies, and my excursions around the nation's capitol. Washington was a bustling town, and though Coolidge was in the White House and the old guard was still in power, it was the younger generation that was setting the tempo. Anything seemed possible during those Jazz Age years of prosperity.

We were an over-eager generation, wanting to shrug off the constrictions of our Victorian parents. World War I had changed things. Even Holton Arms now had military training. We shouldered wooden guns, performed drills, and marched. It was a required activity, but not a popular one. We did not want to think about another war; we wanted to live intensely.

Though I studied hard, I had time for fun. I made the rounds of spring hops, cotillion dances, June Germans, fall proms, mid-winter dances, and spring proms. Any excuse! From West Point to Winston-Salem, a group of us were known as prom-trotters and thought ourselves fortunate to be in that group. Unfortunately, my prom-trotting did not include Princeton or Roge. It did include

16

Harry Manning, my sea captain, who was in touch and in earnest. I was crazy about him, but his intentions for us were more far-reaching than mine, perhaps because he was ten years my senior.

I returned home for the winter holidays and wrote to Roge. My brother, Frank, was sick, and Bluefield seemed cold and isolated. I asked Roge about his novel and whether or not he would be coming back to Princeton. The notion of seeing him again any time soon grew dimmer. I was fascinated by his "writer's life" in California, though, and he was a little in awe of Southern girls for being spell-binding and unusual.

January Ninth
1926

Adorable Mary Lou . . .

Your letter, like the exotic fragrance of old wine, has all but intoxicated me. It is sweet of you, Mary Lou, to remember me after what has seemed so long a time.

I have tried to forget you—it all seems so hopeless—and yet I know I cannot because . . . may I say, because you are too lovely?

But cheerio! If you are blue and lonesome, I must strike a happier note than my own desolation at not being near you. And I shall write often.

Still plugging along at writing, but I haven't hit my stride and the temptation to loaf and say, "Well, I've written enough for today—now for a little golf" is such that I find weeks slipping by without having accomplished anything. What with bridge, golf and occasional parties, I discover a story started two weeks ago to be only half done.

My plans are still somewhat up in the air. It looks very much as though I might return to Princeton next fall—and then again no. At any rate I think we go East by then—California is too delightfully indolent. Here it is early January and instead of a howling blizzard, the sun is blazing wrathfully. A bunch of us went moonlight swimming the other night and it was quite warm.

Sorry to hear Frank is ill. I only met him once or twice, but from that little and what Gordon told me about him, he is one of

17

the finest. He and Dirk Rankin, I used to think, were the apex of—well, what we of the class of 1927 would call in rather subdued voices "a damn good gent."

My class is now 1929—I shall be quite an antique by then— an unsophisticated sophomore while my whilom classmates are gravely looking forward to diplomas with which to conquer the world.

If I don't go back to college, I'll probably try something in New York—newspaper work or bonds or something.

Don't hardly see how you'll be lonesome in Bluefield what with so many colleges around and M.L. looking good enough to eat. You might as well own up to Uncle Roger that Bluefield will only see you between dances. Are you a Charleston expert? I've been hoping desperately it would die out before I had to learn it, but out here they are all crazy about it. So far I have sternly refused to submit—mais, que voulez-vous?

If I go back to Princeton, you'll sure 'nough have to arrange to study something or other in New York and we'll have some noble times. All my friends will be seniors, so I'll have to be wary about letting them know you since a senior is, I understand, a dangerous character. I can already imagine what we'll do. It is, say, Wednesday afternoon. I haven't seen you since the preceding Sunday and am, consequently, suffering agonies. I consume cigarets feverishly and wonder if it is too soon to ring you. Desperate, I call your number.

Me: Are you there, Mary Lou?

You: (charitably) Yes. How're you, Roge?

Me: (immensely cheered) Just noble. A bit crazy, probably, but on the whole . . . Are you doing anything Saturday—um— and Sunday?

You: I'm awfully sorry . . . that's a pretty large order.

Me: (contemplating suicide) Oh, dear!

You: (coldly) Dear?

Me: (in a panic) I mean, that is . . . you see . . .

You: Quite.

Me: I thought . . . well, Gordon and Walt Hale and Johnny Moss—we thought you might . . .

You: Who thought?

Me: You might come down for the game and then we'd all

go to Pierre's.

You: (kindly, taking pity) Well, I might . . .

Me: Angel!

You: Please . . .

Me: I know, I'm sorry, but you are. (carried away) Also adorable, enchanting, beloved, marvelous, wonderful, maddeningly lovely . . .

(A click informs me that you have hung up, but I smile because I know you will forgive me.

Curtain falls with a smash.

Act II

Scene: Princeton. A dormitory room.

Time: 5 P.M.

Weather: A brisk snap is in the air. Football weather.

Five youths and one girl are discovered in a room. A bright fire burns in the fireplace. Gordon McNeer is mixing highballs. Ave Sherry is strumming a banjo. The girl is standing before the fireplace. She has a soft Southern accent and a charming smile. All have just returned from the game.

Gordon: A snifter, Mary Lou?

You: A very small one.

Me: (abstractedly) Isn't she wonderful?

(They all have a highball.)

Moss: A corking game, wasn't it?

Sherry: Great. Tum-tum-da-dee.

You: I thought the Harvard quarterback—

Others: (darkly) Ha!

You:—was terrible.

Others: Ah!

Walt Hale: Shall we eat here or in New York?

Sherry: Here. It's too early to go down yet. I've got to phone Lisbeth and tell her what time we'll pick her up.

(The Others leave on similar errands. You and Me are left alone. We talk gaily until the Others return and the party is on.)

(Author's note: The Others are rushed from the scene for purely selfish reasons, so that Me can talk to You alone.)

And so enough. Wouldn't life be jolly if all our dreams

came true? Please write soon, Mary Lou.

> With much love,
> Roge

> March 15, 1926
> 316 25th Street
> Santa Monica, Calif.

Dear Mary Lou,

I say, how are you, Mary Lou? Wonderful? I knew it! Also . . . (but hold on, old son, you've already tried to tell her that.)

Pardon the soliloquy. I am feeling positively effervescent this morning, the result of a corking swim in the placid waters of the Pacific. It was simply marvelous, although a bit cold till you once got in . . . then—oh, lady!

I've been in about four times this week and it certainly is sterling. I'm getting brown as a nut,—eh? Did I hear something said about only needing the brown? But is is great sport and I'm regaining my youthful figure . . . swim a mile or so up the beach and then run back.

As somebody once remarked—"wish you were here"—but I mean it in all seriousness and then some.

I won't apologize for not writing before—my letters bore you anyway—but tempus certainly does fugit and while I think, in my rare moments of consciousness, and dream, when in my customary foggy state, of you—very enchanting dreams, too—it seems that I never find the requisite energy and paper and pen to sit down and tell you all about it.

But every so often I manage to steam up enough and this letter is partially the result of taking a blonde to the Biltmore in Los Angeles the other night. Well, Mary Lou, you know you have spoiled me for blondes (to say nothing of brunettes, in passing) and when I danced with her I mumbled, "By Jove, you're really not bad at this, but you can't begin to compare with a certain someone down in Bluefield"—and when I looked at her I said, "By Jove, you're rather pretty, you know, but you haven't got golden curls and come-hither-and-worship blue eyes, to say nothing of a cherry-ripe mouth like Mary Lou"— and when she talked I gravely informed her, "Your line is very delightful—no, I mean it—but then, it is harsh and strident when I think of the soft tinkling melody of Mary Lou."

Which, you will say, is absurd. Ah, well—so are most of my thoughts about Mary Lou, absurd yet none the less painful.

But there! I always get so darn morbid—no, that isn't the right word—when I write to you. I come along with both feet on the pathos pedal, hoping, I suppose, to draw a little pity . . . Because you are so far away and a cloudless blue sky in California only reminds me of eyes infinitely more blue and beautiful in Bluefield.

> Ever humbly and—well,
> sincerely, but you know
> what I mean—
> Roge

By that spring, Mrs. Holton realized my sights were still set on Europe. With my parents' approval, she helped me investigate options for my return, and we found the perfect set-up. The fashionable Finch School in New York had an extension program in Versailles. I would be in France and I would be furthering my education, which pleased everyone. By the fall of 1926, I was ready to go.

Chapter 3

I boarded the S.S. *France* and set out across the Atlantic. Harry sent me a wireless as our ships passed at sea. This impressed the captain of the *France*, who invited me to the bridge and let me take hold of the big wheel and steer the ship.

I was bound for Paris, the cultural crossroads of the twenties, home to artists and expatriates and others compelled by their romantic flair. Though I was younger than the "Lost Generation" and not completely in step with their carelessness, I expected to enjoy their efforts in art and music and literature.

I am sure I sent Roge my marvelous new address: Villa des Sorbiers, 19 Avenue Villeneuve d'Etang, Versailles, France. I did not hear from him, though, which gave me pause, but did not slow me down.

Our villa was a beautiful spot with walled grounds and an aura all its own. The Palace of Versailles was close by, and I often rode horseback in the forests and lagoons around it during the early morning. Had Louis XIV and his entourage shown up on one of those dawns, I would not have been surprised. It was very easy to get carried away in such a place where the mist was like a curtain rising on another time.

The Finch School had a fantastic program. Our instructors

told us we were majoring in French and art! Though we lived at the villa, our studies were largely conducted in Paris: academic classes at the Sorbonne, lectures at the Louvre, cooking classes at the Cordon Bleu, art classes at Julians where I sketched nude models.

Our social life was busy with tea dances and chaperoned soirees. Since we were in the world's fashion center, we did lots of shopping and were driven around Paris by our handsome Arab chauffeur named Said. One couturier convinced me to buy a Lanvin ball gown along with a resplendent silver thread wig which was very much in vogue and very extreme.

We also toured Europe in small groups. In Naples, I rose early to watch the December sunrise over the bay and Vesuvius on the day I turned 20. In Rome, I went with a Roman Catholic friend and her family for a private audience with Pope Pius XI.

It was the winter social season in Rome with tea dances and Friday evening galas at the Excelsior Hotel. A friend's father saw to it that we did not miss a single dance by engaging gigolos for the evening. These handsome, young Italians in formal dress would come to our table, bow, and ask us for a dance. My gigolo was a charmer and asked me to show him the Charleston or "Charlie Stone," as he pronounced it. I thought I must tell Roge about this.

It is hard to put in print the exuberance of the time I spent in France and Europe. It was a lush, heavenly world. The more I saw, the more I wanted to know. It was never enough. It was a spree of learning and living, of unbridled enthusiasm for sights and sounds and magical possibilites. This dream I was living had to fade away, as all dreams do, and it was with a mixture of sadness and anticipation that I boarded the S.S. *Conte Biancamano* in Genoa in December of 1926.

The new Italian liner, the *Count of the White Hands*, was carrying many expatriates back to the United States. I met a nice crowd of people my first day on board, including Frank Bateman, who introduced me to the MacKenzie Allens and the Ludlow Fowlers. We played bridge and had a grand time.

The next day I was on the bow of the ship watching Gibraltar go by when I met F. Scott Fitzgerald. He was friendly and easy to meet and very boyish-looking with a sensitive face.

easy to meet and very boyish-looking with a sensitive face. That night, I played bridge again with Frank, the Allens, the Fowlers and Scott. Ludlow Fowler had been Scott's best man when he married Zelda. We ate dinner and danced; I enjoyed myself immensely.

Scott had just turned thirty when I met him, and his promise as a writer seemed immeasurable. In five years, he had written three novels: *This Side of Paradise*, which brought him early success; *The Beautiful and Damned*; and *The Great Gatsby*, his investigation of the American dream and most critically acclaimed work to date. The Scott I met was not a legend; he was a popular writer. He and Zelda were celebrities of the Jazz Age. Zelda was on board, but remained in their stateroom most of the time, leaving their little daughter Scottie to the care of her nanny.

A day or so later, I was on deck and Scott dashed over and asked me to enter a quoits tournament with him. We had a great time and won the game. Afterward, we joined others and talked for three hours. I was spellbound.

Scott was enthusiastic about ideas and people and life, and we had a great rapport. He listened with fascination; you felt as though you were the only person in the world that interested him. Such concentration was like an unspoken compliment, and so I found myself talking to him with ease, and not like a tongue-tied twenty year old in the company of a celebrity.

He liked to say my name—Mary Louise Archer—and told me to call him Scott. He also admired my hair and a little blue hat with violets that I wore. I described him in my journal as "too cute for words!" and added, "He seems to like me— and flatters me anyway. Rather pleases me." I was enamored.

In the evenings, Scott liked to get together with the literary types on board as well as other people he knew. Since Zelda was in no shape to join him, he asked me if I would like to be his hostess and have meals with him when he entertained. I readily accepted his invitation, though it had to be cleared with my chaperone first.

My chaperone could not refuse his charm and really was proud to have one of "her girls" so honored. The only problem was that she could not let me be in the bar for the drinks before dinner. Scott immediately worked this out by having a special place set up outside the bar where his guests could bring their drinks.

Scott arranged to meet me early before my first dinner as hostess so that he could fill me in on the background of his guests. If they were writers, he discussed their books so that I would be informed. Some I had read, and some I had not. He briefed me thoroughly on his guests because he wanted me to be comfortable in conversation with them.

Thanks to his thoughtful preparation, I was able to hold my own. The British novelist Francis Brett Young was a regular guest. He was on his way to the states to promote his latest book, *Love is Enough*. (At the end of his lecture tour in the states, he came to visit me in Bluefield.) I also met Joseph Hergesheimer, another novelist whose books often explored the decadent lifestyle of the very wealthy.

I looked forward to each and every evening—cocktails, conversation, and dancing with Scott and the others. They were all lovely to me. To one fancy dress party, I wore a Spanish shawl and mantilla and noted that I was one of the few not married. They were a fast, young married set, and it was a very gay party.

I was thrilled to be included in these wonderful evenings, all thanks to Scott. He wanted to know about me and my background and my feelings on subjects. His curiosity was boundless, his energy fueled by a romantic flame full of hope. I did not know then that alcoholism was already a real threat to his well-being, as well as the strain of his marriage to Zelda. It would be nine long years before he would finish another book.

The last few days on board were windy and rough, and we were all glad to see New York and be on terra firma after two weeks at sea. The newspapers were full of the Fitzgeralds' return; they had been abroad for more than two years. It was hard to break away from such glamorous company. Luckily, Scott's cousins, the Taylor girls of Norfolk, were friends of mine, and since he visited them with some frequency, we said farewell knowing we would probably meet again.

I was at Virginia Beach the following summer when Scott visited Cecilia Taylor and her children. I rode horseback in the morning on the beach, where Scott and I would meet to sit in the work in Hollywood, though he did not like it much. He was great company, and we were happy to see each other again.

My time in France and my voyage home had been more than I could have imagined. I feel certain that I wrote to Roge about my adventures, but then again I might have been too busy. We had not been in touch for over a year. Another year would fly by before I heard from him. Though Bluefield was my home address, it seems I was always packing my bag to visit somebody somewhere. I was often in demand as a bridesmaid. I travelled a great deal to New York, where I had friends from Finch, and to the college parties in Virginia and North Carolina.

The parties were fun, sometimes on the wild side, but since I did not drink much I got to drive the car most of the time. I did smoke; most everybody did in those days. I smoked in front of my father, but I never considered lighting up a cigarette in front of Mother.

On one memorable trip to The Breakers in Palm Beach with a Finch friend, I decided to take the big step. I had my long, curly hair cut off into a bob. This was not just a haircut; it was a declaration. It was hard to get used to my new self, but I was accustomed to my lack of hair by the time I returned to Bluefield. My parents were, in a word, shocked. I was not punished, but endured severe looks for many days.

I performed another reckless act on my way home from a wedding in Dayton, Ohio. My escort from the wedding was driving me to Cincinnati to catch a train to Bluefield when we noticed a sign advertising airplane rides—$20 for twenty minutes. A dollar a minute was steep by 1927 standards, but this young fellow and I were intrigued by the idea of flying. Only a handful of people had been airborne. We decided to investigate.

The pilot was sitting in a small shed on the edge of a harvested cornfield. After a short discussion, we decided to go up. My escort said, "Ladies first," so the pilot handed me a leather helmet with goggles and a snappy white scarf.

The plane was a two-seater with an open cockpit. My seat was behind the pilot, who strapped me in carefully with a heavy harness. Once the pilot was in his seat, he signalled his helper, who pulled on the propeller. We bumped over to a cleared spot, raced down the dirt runway, and climbed into the air. It was fantastic.

We climbed higher still and then did a loop-the-loop. Before I knew what had happened, we went upside down and around and pulled out of it. It took my breath away; I loved it.

The last maneuver—the falling leaf—finally scared me. We climbed high into the sky and then did a nose dive straight down with the plane turning round and round, like a falling leaf. The earth came closer with each turn until I thought we would crash. At the last possible moment, or so I thought, the pilot pulled the plane out of its tumbling and we zoomed up again.

My escort went up for the same ride. I sat by the shed, leaned back, and watched the plane. The perspective from the ground wa impossibly different. We thanked the pilot for the adventure and paid him for the thrill.

446 - 26th Street
Santa Monica
Jan. 8, 1928

Mary Lou—dearest,

I am moved to write to you tonight. Ask the stars why—an old memory, a thought back to the happiest time in my life . . . and a picture of golden curls such as I have never seen again, nor ever will—an echo of tinkling laughter and the only time I wished I were a better man—a persistent throb that said, "She is lovely; she is far more than divine . . . "

For I worshipped you very sincerely, Mary Lou. A rather terrifying sincerity, because I was immensely young and believed some kind of fate had hurled us together—and that I should never lose you, as I have done.

Mary Lou, I am a little ashamed—or else terribly proud—that I brooded over you for many inconsolable hours after you had left Princeton. I said, to old Waltuh Hale, inadvertently, "My God, she should never have come!" And I'm afraid I raved, for— for weeks after—whenever I came into Walter's room, he bellowed, "My God! She should never have come!" Because I was known as something of a misogynist and then you came to teach me that—I don't know how to say it, Mary Lou, except that you were a hell of a good sport!

Mother and I leave for Paris within the next few weeks. God knows how we'll go—probably by freight, for I am broke. At any rate, we're both tired of living in California and I've never lived more that three years in one place in my life—so the wanderlust has me and we're off. I cannot stick the idea of camping on one spot forever, although (a sign of impending old age) I rather fear giving up a good job and barging out into the unknown . . .

I suppose some day I'll write, but I've found it impossible while working on the newspaper here. I come home at night, sit down with a firm resolve to pound out a story that's been working in my mind, write a few paragraphs . . . then brain-fog gets me.

I have no idea what I'll do in Paris—probably try my hand at stories, unmolested by the thought of clattering keys and grinding presses left behind.

I think it should be very jolly.

Please write soon, Mary Lou.

Ever, with love,
Roger

It was a lovely letter, and I was so pleased to hear from my friend. I put it with the others, believing that our fascination with each other had finally found its proper niche. Roge was now off to Paris, hopefully to write that book, and I was engaged to be married in November. Our lives seemed on course, and I knew our paths would cross happily down the road.

Chapter 4

This morning I was walking slowly through my new apartment and caught a glimpse of myself in a mirror. My first thought was, "Well, you are finally as old as the hills." My second thought was, "I wonder how Roge would describe you now!" Favorably, I hope. I came of age during the Roaring Twenties, and there is still something of the Jazz Age in me and a cloche hat in my closet.

I no longer have the energy of those days, though, and on this cold winter morning I am particularly creaky and worn. The move from my Charlottesville home of twenty-five years to Williamsburg was exhausting. It was the right decision for my future and "assisted living" is not the bad word I thought it was. We are all assisted in living anyway, by choice or chance, by nursing aides or doctors, husbands or children, by those friends who carry you over the inevitable rough spots. Friends like Roge.

It is a funny thing, memory, and how it is triggered by a smell or a song or the feeling that you have had this feeling before. I have kept journals since I was able to write, so my life is revealed to me by my own hand. I like to compare how I saw it then to how I see it now. Time does not necessarily make you heal or forget, even when you are eighty-eight years old, but it does make you remember differently.

From my stack of journals, unpacked once more last night, I pick up a small leather book. The title page, in my handwriting, says *Thoughts: October 1924 - January 1927.* In this half-full journal, I find poetry and prose that must have interested me. Dashes of Shakespeare and Socrates, Byron and Yeats, Schopenhauer and Edna St. Vincent Millay, and lots of quotes unattributed. I was young and unencumbered and trying to forge my own raison d'etre.

One anonymous quote intrigues me. "We must not expect too much from life, but learn to accommodate ourselves to a world where all is relative and no perfect state exists." I understand this perfectly now, but in 1927 I am sure I did not believe it. Such a pragmatic prescription for life would not have been my philosophy when the world was accommodating me.

I married soon after I abandoned writing great thoughts in this little book. November 24, 1928. Edward Temple Ryland was from an old Richmond family and was five years older than I was. He was handsome and fun and already associated in business with the Albemarle Paper Company when I met him. That worked in his favor with me. I was a bit weary of college boys.

The paper company had offices in Richmond and New York, and we chose New York. After our wedding, we lived in an apartment on Park Avenue and then at Forest Hills on Long Island. It was a booming time with lots of friends and a young marriage full of promise and hope.

In the spring, we gloried in the news that I was going to have a baby. In October, the stock market crashed on Black Tuesday, and the Roaring Twenties evaporated. The office called Ed back to Richmond. Mary Louise was born. Ed lost his job, but quickly found employment with a life insurance company.

Life in Richmond was pleasant and familiar, but the Depression was a serious thing and we all had losses and cutbacks. My second daughter, Temple, arrived in 1932. Ed and I continued with a bustling social life, but life at home was becoming strained.

I went to Virginia Beach often during those summers, and saw Scott Fitzgerald a couple of times. One meeting was without advance notice. I went to a party, and he was there. It was a surprise for both of us, and we were glad to see each other. He looked much older and careworn. He was living in Baltimore at the time.

Scott was struggling to complete another novel, but Zelda's breakdowns were taking their toll on him. He was deeply concerned about Scottie, and his dissipation from alcohol was bad. He was awfully glad to see me, and we stayed together all evening. People at the party wondered about us; they did not know that we already knew each other.

The next time I saw Scott was the summer after *Tender is the Night* was finally published. For a Depression-year novel, it sold well, but the sales did not come up to Scott's expectations. His careless expatriates of the twenties were no longer a popular subject in the dark days of the Depression. Scott gave me a copy of *Tender*, which he signed with the inscription: "To Mary Lou, with memories of the Conte Biancomano and Virginia Beach. From her admirer, F. Scott Fitzgerald." That was 1934.

A year or so later, matters were such that my marriage could not continue. Our relationship had become unstable, which was not good for the children, and there was no hope for future restoration.

It was hard to leave on many levels. I had many friends in Richmond and was sad to say good-bye to them. I worried about Mary Lou and Tempie. I also worried about myself and my future. Divorce is never an easy solution, though sometimes it is necessary. The children and I returned to Bluefield to live with my parents, and I made plans to travel to Reno. Nevada then, as now, was the state of the expedited divorce.

July fourteenth 1935
Bluefield, W. Va.

Dear Roge,

Am planning to be in California in September so naturally thought of you and what fun it would be to see you again after all these years. No doubt you are married at this point, and if so would love to see you and meet your wife.

Am leaving tonight for Reno and after my decree will be with an aunt of mine in Los Angeles for a short time before returning East.

This address of yours is probably all wrong by now but hope you receive this.

My address for the next six weeks will be Washoe Pines Ranch, Franktown, Nevada via Carson City.

So here's hoping I shall get to see you—

Mary Lou Archer Ryland

The train trip to Nevada was long with frequent stops, but it was a relief to be on my way after months of worry and a harassed state of mind. In Chicago, I switched to the "Overland Limited," a top-notch, transcontinental train, very long and brightly lit and air-conditioned, which kept us all from perishing in the desert heat.

I passed the time reading or sketching and talking to other passengers, many of whom were on their way to California. I had a queer feeling of being ashamed at getting off at Reno, so I told my companions I was going to a dude ranch for a visit. I am sure I looked guilty, and they knew. But by the time the train reached Reno, there were many good-byes and good luck wishes for my future.

It was dark when I arrived, and I was met by the daughter of the couple who ran the ranch. With her were three cowboys (or hands) from the ranch, who helped with the luggage. We all piled into a bus-like automobile and drove twenty-five miles out in the night to the Washoe Pines Ranch.

The ranch was a choice place to stay, and there were many guests there. The couple who owned it were from the East and had built up a wonderful reputation over the years. It was a working ranch, and we watched the cowboys in rodeo, roping calves and riding steers. Once we were familiar with our cowpony and a Western saddle, we went on camping trips, sometimes riding thirty to forty miles a day.

Life at the ranch was never boring. In the evenings, we sometimes staged theatricals. Mostly though, we enjoyed the outdoors and exercise and good food, so it was a healthy environment. The physical regimen was invigorating and certainly helped our emotional well-being. We did not languish.

Guests were coming and going according to when it was their time to go to court. There was a great variety of people at the ranch. The diversity was fascinating and all the more curious because we shared the common goal of getting a divorce. We would not have been at the Washoe Pines Ranch for any other reason but a failed marriage. The past, present, and the future seemed to converge, and we were all coping with such a vortex.

I was apprehensive about Mary Lou and Tempie and stayed in frequent touch. The polio epidemic was in full force that summer, and many friends had suffered the death of a child from the disease. Others had children who had been crippled. My parents kept the girls inside most of the time and watched them closely.

Finally, it was my day in court. I was given gardenias, which was something of a tradition, and drove into town with my resident witness. My lawyer, who had visited me periodically during the six weeks, was waiting for us. I though a great deal of him. He was a dear, older man and very compassionate.

We appeared before the judge, who questioned me, as did my lawyer. I had to swallow hard with each answer to keep from being choked up, even though my answers were simple statements and the questions were being asked kindly. The process was easy and short, but the emotions were hard. My marriage to Edward was dissolved. It took eight minutes to dissolve my almost seven year marriage, and I emerged feeling numb and relieved.

It seemed fitting to be in Reno, the West, the frontier land where the American spirit had been challenged and forged anew. I went to a bridge over the Truckee River thinking of what had happened and what was yet to be. There was a poignant tradition of buying an inexpensive wedding ring to throw into the river after receiving your decree. I wondered how many women had stood in my spot and watched the current carry away the cheap imitation. I dropped mine and watched it plop and disappear. It was done; gone down the river. I stepped off the bridge onto a dusty road and saw a sign that said, "No Speed Limit. Drive Safely."

Chapter 5

With my decree in hand, I boarded the train for Los Angeles the next day. I looked forward to being in California—a sunny transition before returning home. My aunt and I had a lovely time, and I had loads of fun with friends in San Francisco and San Diego. I wondered vaguely about Roge. He had not contacted me while I was at the ranch. I knew my note to him had been a long shot. He might not have received it since the address I used was ancient. But perhaps he did receive it and did not want to be in touch. Sometimes the past is the past. Part of mine was certainly over.

I packed my bags and headed home to West Virginia. It was grand to see Mary Lou and Tempie, and I was anxious to get on with the business of living.

We settled comfortably into my parents' home and found a familiar routine which was good for the girls. It was a relief to be out from under the stress of a failing marriage.

I was a divorced mother with children, which did not qualify me for the mainstream, especially in Bluefield. I did not feel out of step, however. I simply had a new set of circumstances, and I was determined to make things work. My daughters were a source of strength; I had to be strong for them as we smoothed the ground between before and after.

That ground, that road was uncharted, and though the sign had said "No Speed Limit. Drive Safely," I was often unsure of which way to go. Crossroads are always difficult. I wondered if I had corrected the problem and begun a better course or just made a new tangle of worries.

While at the ranch, I had written to friends explaining my new situation, and their encouraging replies were waiting for me on my dressing table. Included in the pile of letters was my letter to Roge. It had been returned, addressee unknown. I found out from someone or another, probably our Princeton matchmaker Gordon McNeer, that Roge had gone to London with the Associated Press. It was terrific news, a plum of a job for Roge. He was in the big league.

I had written to him in July knowing I would be in California and hoping he might still be there and wouldn't it be fun to see him. I had no real reason to write him again; there was little chance of seeing him now that he was in London. But, I had thought of him off and on over the years, wondering what he was up to, and occasionally smiling about our Princeton weekend together. Curiosity compelled me to try one more time, and I dashed off a note to Roger Greene, Associated Press Foreign Staff, London.

It was now September, and I watched the sunlight heighten the color of the mountains as I walked to the post office one afternoon. The postman handed me the bundle.

"There's a letter for you, " he said with a wink.

"Oh, good," I replied.

He leaned over the counter and in whispered amazement added, "All the way from London, England."

I thumbed through the bundle immediately and found a letter with the return address: Roger D. Greene, The Associated Press, Hind Court, Fleet Street, London, England.

"Oh, thank you," I said to the postman and rushed home, paying no more attention to the mountain scenery.

Hind Court
Fleet Street
London, September 17, 1935

Dear Mary Lou:

If ever I heard a cry from the wilderness that thrilled me deep down, it was and is your letter—the familiar Mary Lou handwriting, the same blue paper and the long-remembered old address "131 Monroe Street, Bluefield, W. Va."

Good Lord!

Well, the trans-Atlantic cables couldn't tell it quick enough—the bursting, dancing star-shells that your letter touched off. I had just come back to the office after a five-day junket down on the south coast, breaking a sweet "scoop" on the British home fleet steaming out secretly for Gibraltar ready for Mussolini—with not another newspaper man on the scene—and there in my mailbox was the blue envelope and "Mr. Roger D. Greene, Associated Press Foreign Staff" on it in handwriting that sent an old, sweet nostalgia flooding back.

I took it quietly. Very calm. I didn't let out the war-whoop I felt busting inside. I didn't say hello to the bunch in the office; I shook hands with them sort of numbly, back on the job again after my expedition, and went to a desk in a corner where I could be alone to read your letter; and I read it and read it over and over again. So after a while I called, "Boy—copy!" and slammed a sheet in a typewriter and knocked off a lot of sudden nonsense and tore it up and finally arrived at something pretty prosaic, and hollered for a cable-boy. He was still there. I said fiercely, "Get that off—quick!" and he was off like a streak to the nearest teletype and batting away at the keys for dear life while I stood over him glowering.

I had to write a feature story after that, and it was the hardest story I ever wrote. My mind simply was not on it. I was, suddenly, 3000 miles away and ten years ago . . . back at college, at Princeton Junction, standing on the platform the day before the "frosh" prom, in a fever of nervousness, meeting this fabulous Mary Lou Archer about whom I had heard such lyrical adoration, simply terrified, and "Waltuh" (Hale) only made it worse when he drawled something about, "Yo' colluh is up around yo' ear. What you

39

fidgetin' about?"—just when I was furiously practicing ennui and how a sophomore would act.

So the train stopped and you came radiantly down the steps in a tricky gray traveling suit and miraculous curls and a bright, quick smile and laughing eyes and a Southern accent that mortally wounded me. I was slain; I was as good as dead, and it is a wonder that somebody didn't come down and take me by the hand and say, "Boy, you better lie down. Your heart has clean stopped!"

A long time ago . . .

And now an old song goes whirling endlessly through my head, as it did then and for long after. You remember:—

. . . all the chimes in the steeple
Are waiting to ring,
And all the people . . .

I never heard it, for three or four or more years, without a sort of dull pain in the heart and a crowding lot of memories of one short weekend in life which was the sum and total of our being together.

Then I heard of your wedding, and a card came saying Mr. and Mrs. Ryland would be at home at something Roseneath Avenue, and I thought, "Well, so that's life, fella, and how have you been?" "All right—until now," I answered darkly, because that's the way life is—that your marriage shocked me. I couldn't explain why it did. There it was, no rime or reason, but there it was—an inescapable fact.

Well, Mary Lou, there is so much to say. So darn much has happened. I love the way you decided to write me a very proper note to the old Santa Monica address and added, "no doubt you have a charming wife by now, and I would love to see you both!!" You could only have seen "us both," Mary Lou, if you had had a good many mint juleps, because I have been too busy whirling around and about the terrestrial premises, almost ever since I last saw you, to get married. I've come within an eyebrow of it twice, but on both occasions, just when I was fluttering around with the large idea, on the very verge and all that, a sudden twist of fate or whatever you want to call it stepped in and sent me pursuing this fatal newspaper career to the other side of the continent. From Santa Monica to New York, where I spent more than a year on the N. Y. Herald Tribune—then back to Santa Monica, to San Francisco, and nine months ago to London. I left New York, in 1931, because I was hitting the pulp magazines in a big way, selling stories I wrote between working hours as fast as I could bat them out. So I left the H-Trib, thinking, "I am an author! My typewriter is my desk. I'll go back to California and gather fame in the sunshine." I stopped writing pulpies (too degradingly vulgar) and turned to the "slicks" —the smooth paper publications such as the SatEvePost, Colliers, Liberty, etc. I sold two stories to Liberty and one movie scenario ("The Devil is Driving," starring Edmund Lowe) and did a lot of plain and fancy starving for two years on those lean returns.

It was, looking back, pretty funny—a long story, but these were the high-lights: actually hungry and painfully hungry living in a $200-a-month bachelor suite in the best apartment house in Santa Monica, so desperately poor that I smuggled groceries in by my fire-escape window and cooked them on an electric-grill, quaking lest the manager should hear me, almost suffocated by the smoke of burning chops, in my dressing room—and many times drinking hot water for dinner to keep me awake while I wrote. All this time I was—or so they said—the "amusing" fella of a crowd of movie writers and stars . . . Doris Kenyon, Lew Cody, Theda Bara, Nat Pendleton, Richard Bennett, Spenser Tracy, Warren Williams, Frank Borzage, Joel McCrea, Irene Rich, Anita Loos, Agnes Christine Johnstone, etc. I used to play tennis in the afternoon with Doris Kenyon and her satellites four or five days a week when I was so damn hungry I dined en route to her court on tangerines and pomegranates. I've been to countless cocktail parties at delightful Theda Bara's chateau in Beverly Hills when the hors d'oeuvres found me a more fascinated customer than the crowded bar where two Senegalese boys were madly shaking up Theda's potent absinthe cocktails by the gallons. And many times I sallied forth all gay and immaculate in evening dress to the Mayfair movie ball or to a premiere, with microphones and thousands gaping at each privileged entrant, with the air of a very bored, very rich young man and neither a penny in my lovely trouser pockets nor a bread-crumb in the howling torment of my inner man.

In short, I ultimately came to the decision that free-lance writing was glamorous but extremely painful on the tissues. I made one last effort. I went into complete hibernation in a little town outside Los Angeles called Whittier, hired a funny little cottage for $8 a month, raised ducks, shocked the Quaker populace into holding prayer-meetings for me by painting my front door a violent and scandalous crimson—Chinese lacquer—and worked 18 hours a day batting out a great many thousands of words for Liberty Weekly's $10,000 first-novel contest, won sixth place out of 28,000 manuscripts submitted—but no money.

And so, pretty sick of hungry starving, I went back to newspaperdom.

That was weird, too. The way it was timed, as though some kind of a god was mischievously watching over my destiny. It was late July. An old Andover school-mate, Dick Allen, who was broke too, had come over to stay with me at the "Greene Chateau with the Red Door." We had spent all his last $16 on food, all but a lone dollar. We packed blankets and frying pans and set off on a hike down the beach. We were gone four days, sleeping out under the stars and having a glorious time, plotting our future. We decided to go back to the "Greene chateau" until the rent was up, a week later, kill the rest of my ducks for food, and then set out on a vagabond trip around the world—first down through Mexico, then hop a tramp ship to the South Seas, thence to the Malay Archipelago, to China, Russia and all around. That was July, 1933.

This sounds, I know, like a phantasmagore; but—just as we were all set to sally forth, the proverbial last-minute telegram came. It was from my former boss in Santa Monica, who had since become publisher of the San Francisco Call-Bulletin, wanting to know if I would accept a job up there, and enclosing fifty dollars. And it was the first time I had heard from him in more than a year!

Well, Dick and I celebrated. We went out and cashed the Western Union money order, and went to the market and bought the two biggest T-bone steaks in the world, and a quart of wine. I left Dick all except my boat-fare to San Francisco, and twelve hours later I was back in the Fourth Estate—these so-called "Gentlemen of the Press."

A year there in delightful San Francisco, where I became the ace re-write man on the biggest afternoon paper and had a magnificent time . . . living in a pent-house atop Russian Hill with another scribe and a Mark Hopkins hotel "crooner" who was the local Bing Crosby—and then the London venture, starting last November.

So it has been an eventful life since I last saw you, Mary Lou, in the cloistered halls of Princeton and the Sunday afternoon in that New York chop-suey joint where they must, I know, have played horrible music but it sounded divine to me and I forgot everything except dancing with you.

I've got to stop now. A pretty large day tomorrow. But please, Mary Lou, will you write me all about yourself quick, and did you ever think of coming to England because I seem to be billeted here for quite a while.

Ever and anon,
Roge

Chapter 6

More than seven years had gone by since I had held a letter from Roge, and I could not let go of this one. I read it two or three times, and then lay back on my bed and looked out the window, over the mountains, past the shore, and across the Atlantic.

My short, polite note to him had "thrilled him deep down." I had not thrilled anybody of late, I was sure of that. Divorce in 1935 was not commonplace, and nobody was thrilled about it.

But here was Roge, not questioning why I got married or why I got divorced or why my life seemed to be a quandary. His vote was in my favor when the world was undecided.

I wrote back to him that night. My letter was full of questions about the glamorous life of a foreign correspondent. His parents must have been so proud of him; his talent was being recognized. I imagined the newsroom, the typewriters, the copy boy, Roge pounding out a story posthaste.

And I liked the idea of feeling connected to that life because Roge might think of me while he walked down a London street. I liked the way he saw me. I liked thinking about the girl with golden curls who went to Princeton for a dance.

That girl was not me anymore, and though I liked being reminded of her, I thought Roge should see me now, eleven years older and a mother to boot. I enclosed two photographs in my letter. One was taken at the Washoe Pines Ranch. I was in chaps and holding a 10-gallon hat, ready for a pack trip. I thought it would amuse him.

I mailed my letter and waited and watched my children. I wrote him again, hoping he would write back.

Hampstead Heath
October 19, 1935

Dear Mary Lou:

The leaves begin to fall, red-brown and gold and glorious. The fog seeps in, like the white breath of a ghost. And the rains come pattering down in monotone, chill and dreary. But my coal-fire is warm and glowing, and I hug its warmth without heed to the wind soughing mournfully over Hampstead Heath . . .

And maybe that's the way to begin this letter—to talk about something sane like the weather when my mind is so full of tumult after your letter.

There are so many thousand things to say—whole chapters about the two pictures of you, the first image I have had of you since that bleak day in 1924 when the frosh prom was swept into the dust-bin of time and I was left, pretty miserable and forlorn amidst Princeton's so-called "cloistered halls" while you rippled back to a placed called Bluefield which I had never known but which seized immediately in my mind as the embodiment of all adventure and all romance. Bluefield! Why, good Lord! How I used to dream of you, Mary Lou, and try to picture the town and how you graced it, and Waltuh Hale's soft Southern accent only cruelly reminding me of you until, in despair, I'd go back to my "digs" and try to think up lyrical things to write you while my elder brother, Bill, chuckled up behind his book: "What's the matter, boy—you got heart-burn?" He was pretty depressing.

I don't suppose I've changed much. I haven't had time; I've been too busy. And it alarms me. I feel I should get gruff and hugely serious about life, but I can't. I see my old school-mates and college-mates settled into a stiff collar behind a jowl and a sombre scowl, and they bore me. Yet I wonder, "Good God, ain't you never goin' to grow up?" Maybe. I want to. But, it seems a long way off . . . and that's probably why I became a newspaper man, because there I don't have to fit into the grim mold of business and get all serious, but instead find a vibrant worldliness, and excitement, an intensely tense sense of " this minute counts" which doesn't demand the sober "I-am-a broker" visage of other modes of living. A new day, a new edition, tomorrow.

It's a golden calf I worship, this newspaper game, but I do love it—and with reason. But about that, more later.

I want to talk first about the two snapshots of you, Mary Lou, and the zest I get out of seeing your pretty damn sweet, if you will forgive the words, personal belongings such as smile and eyes and a certain amount of teeth-work which is pretty swell. But, Lord! I have raved about you for ten years now—in Chicago, Los Angeles, New York and lately London. I have told dowagers with starry-eyed but matrimonial daughters, since 1924, that my heart went south on a certain spring, sometime long ago . . .

The rain, now, is hammering down. It comes in gusts, crashing in frenzy on the rooftop, beating madly, then drifting away into a gentle, soporific song . . .

Like life.

I have no picture to send you, Mary Lou, in return for yours. The last one taken was in San Francisco, at the Mark Hopkins, on New Year's Eve 1934, when a news camera-chappie caught me hoisting champagne at a table with Prince Luis Ferdinand of Prussia, grandson of the Kaiser—tight as a drum and looking simply worried to death about the "lead" on my next morning's story; because I was supposed to be the "star" feature writer of the paper and was supposed to be out gathering color material for a sparkling feature yarn on "New Year's Eve in the Town of Towns." And I'd met Prince "Lulu," as he likes to be called, and we got pretty blotto—so much so that I wrote what they afterwards told me was one of the most brilliant pieces ever written about San Francisco night life, but I don't remember writing it at all, and judging by the furrows in my brow when the photographer came along at midnight, I must have been fiercely soured on life. You know Rodin's "The Thinker" and how he has got a good deal of fretwork on the brow, but he was just a piker at fretting compared to R. Denise Greene on New Year's Eve 1934.

I move into a new flat, just around the corner from Westminster Abbey, next week and maybe I'll dig up this infamous panegyric on the Greene countenance and send it to you. Meanwhile, "He was," they said, "a serio-comic lad with a bitter, trenchant humor. He neglects whatever God gave him for a brain, and goes tilting at the windmills of life. He is a dreamer of dreams."

October 31

Your second letter today! And mine neither finished nor posted. God knows, now, why I broke off up above—maybe dreaming of dreams! That's eleven days ago, and a world of things have happened since then; up in Scotland for a week on a story, and since returning, getting settled in the new flat—very sweet, with cherry-glowing coal fires to take the slow-seeping bite out of the fog which is now beginning to roll in, but with ancient plumbing, so that you have to light a gadget called a geyser (pronounced "geezer") over the bathtub to draw hot water—just like the medieval chambers I had last year in old Lincoln's Inn, built in 1415 A.D., and the plumbing original.

Please forgive me for being so damn slow about answering, Mary Lou, though I imagine by the long-delayed time you receive this you will draw up your shoulders and say, "Who is this strange being? Have I heard of him?" Or, no, you won't; you'll just shrug, with that old hot Southern blood rising fast and probably send your seconds around to demand satisfaction, suh!

You know, Mary Lou, there is something pretty gorgeous about you that has lasted a long time. I was terribly excited when your first letter came. I bored every famous American foreign correspondent in London and their wives with hour-long details of "the loveliest, smartest, prettiest kid from down South way you ever heard of, yes, suh! Why, dammit all—" When I had finished, they were swooning like so many dying fish.

I delight in one of your opening paragraphs, Mary Lou, that you "shall not be the elusive person one should be, but waive all formalities, for it is such fun to write when you feel like it." Good God! Don't, please don't, be either elusive or formal. I guess maybe after a long time in this newspaper racket you do get cynical, though I don't see why with life forever giving you its freshest colors, but perhaps I have gotten a little cynical about formality—not decorum, but about the needless "stiffness" which has come to mean the same as formality. And this unwanted, unfelt frigidity and elusiveness which have become the dueling weapons of men against women and women against men, in brief, appall me. It seems so senseless—unless you really mean it. Then, what a formidable weapon!

I didn't know John Herndon at college, though Hugh, being Waltuh Hale's room-mate, was one of my best friends. But "Boots" Converse from Gawgia, sounds very familiar. Was she ever up around Boston way? As a shy junior at Andover, I was introduced by my idol, Bob Allen, captain of the track team, to a stunning Southern gal named "Boots" Converse—whom he jilted, and afterwards regretted so bitterly doing so! I haven't seen John over here, didn't even see Hugh during the year I was in New York. This London is a whirl anyway, leaving little time for whizzing around making new friends. We work hard, play hard, drink hard, read history, blaspheme the British, bewail our soaring golf scores—and wonder, a little wistfully, whether we are as famous foreign correspondents as our friends sometime write us. And if so, what the hell? In this last week, I've had letters from seven different towns, from people I knew and have long since lost from sight; from Tamara Andreeva, a lovely and fiercely intellectual white Russian I knew in San Francisco; from dear Bennie Jeffries in Brentwood, Calif., a grand friend if there ever was one, even though she called me "Uncle Roger" and got married and divorced and then sometimes lifted her lips in a way that made me call "Uncle!"—from Marge Thayer, in Whittier, who is huskily pretty and runs a magazine; from Ben Robertson, a grand lad with whom I toiled on the Herald Tribune in New York in 1930-31; from my Iron Duke, my dad of all persons! in Portland, Oregon, whom I've neither seen nor heard from in 10 years, and so on down the line—all having seen my by-line on London stories, yet not one of them bringing me the sudden thrill that came from the lovely lass who stepped down on the platform at Princeton Junction one Friday afternoon and stepped up off the platform onto a Bluefield-bound train 48 hours later, and that was the last seen by Greene of the lovely Mary Lou!

I drove down through your West Virginia mountains on my way back to California in 1931, knew you were somewhere in Roseneath Avenue a long way off, and hurried on—down through the upper reaches of Florida, Mississippi, Louisiana, Texas and so on out to the coast. I've driven across the continent five times, but by far and away the most glorious is the South. The West I used to tell you about is good, but nothing has ever fascinated me so much as the whole "showboat" picture of the South. I'm a damn Yankee, but I want to live my easy last years and die in the South. "Bring me 'nother mint julep, Herkimer—'cose at last, I'm a man from the South!"

The years to come . . .

Now it's all brisk Yankee drive and bustle, cracking out a career.

But, look, Mary Lou, please don't go and talk about driving a hundred miles to see a football game, on account of that's the one thing that makes me want to throw all these Englishers overboard and paddle this island 3000 miles across the ocean and anchor it somewhere off the coast of New Jersey while I go and help myself to about an hour and a half of gridironics. I don't dare to even look at football scores over here; they make me so damn homesick it takes a whole squad of Scotland Yard's finest to stop me from jumping into the Thames, hitting a high-beat Australian crawl down the river to Southampton, and from there on setting out in good earnest.

An anxious voice called the cable-desk Monday and asked, "How did Yale come out in football?" and I thundered back, "How did your Aunt Emma come out from the privy?" and then I cracked the telephone receiver into small bits and slowly ate it. I mean to say, Mary Lou, a man can stand so much, and thereafter it is simply a shambles.

Well, goodbye, Mary Lou. Please write soon.

Immeasurably,

Roge

Roge had never mentioned his father, and the "Iron Duke" moniker hinted at a reason. I called my father "Big Daddy" and with affection. He was tall and kind with the good looks of an

Englishman and a terrific sense of humor. He was also a businessman and the mining supply company he had begun around 1910 had grown into a large and thriving operation.

Big Daddy believed that modern women should know business. His own mother had taken over the family's retail coal operation when her husband, the British-born Thomas Archer, died in 1878. My father was only three years old at the time. Though he longed to have known his father, Big Daddy and his brothers grew up with a working mother and a caring, responsible sister. The happy result was that he treated women with respect and admiration.

He was indulgent with me, but also disciplined because he wanted me to stand on my own two feet. So, upon returning from Nevada, I followed his suggestion to learn business, a big departure from my liberal arts education.

I enrolled in the local business school and took the courses in bookkeeping, typing, and shorthand. I hated shorthand, but soon became a capable typist, thanks to hours of practice typing up the fine print on stock certificates supplied by Big Daddy. I became well-versed with the office equipment in use at the time.

I enjoyed learning about the business world and imagined being a part of it as a secretary or something more. I imagined having my own business and searched Big Daddy's *New York Times* for clues and ideas. I imagined many plots and scenarios to fill in the gaps in my life.

I also used the paper to determine the sail dates of ships heading for England. There was no airmail in those days, and letters could take several weeks to cross "the pond." To assure a quicker crossing, I sent letters to Roge by way of a specified ship. At the bottom of the envelope, I would write "Via S.S. *Europa*. Sail date 10/24/35." Our postman enjoyed this detail, just as he enjoyed waving a letter from London when I walked into the post office.

Roge's letters came back via this ship or that. The girl in Bluefield and the man in England writing about their times by way of one meeting on one weekend long before. It was a story Roge could write, and I reminded him of the novel he had envisioned when we drank early morning milk near Princeton Junction. A novel, he said, that would include me.

20 Tudor Street
London November 23, 1935

Mary Lou my dear:

I have never been happier than tonight. Your letters sort of thrill me. Sort of? Good lord! they tumble my heart and bring back an old sweet hunger I had almost forgotten since long and long ago. And so today, a whizzing Cockney office lad cried, "Mile, sir!" and handed your letter across my desk, taking me instantly 3000 miles away from Hitler and Mussolini and the madness of Europe I was feverishly struggling to write about. You simply ruin the Greene typewriter tempo; for the rest of the day I pecked desultorily away at the keys, a washout, with Hitler and Mussolini and Europe all at once becoming not important at all . .

Dreams, my dear fellow, dreams. And it may be so. But I like to think of you, Mary Lou, and dream—even so.

I like the way G. K. Chesterfield put it:

When all my days are ending
  And I have no song to sing,
I think I shall not be too old
  To stare at everything:
As I stared once at a nursery door
  Or a tall tree and a swing!

It seems to me he meant that the rushing, busy years of grown-up life, the frowning serious pursuit of business, are not worth quite so much as the wondering glimpses of beauty in childhood—"as I stared once at a nursery door, or a tall tree and a swing." And, sentimental or not, as I stared once at the dancing, laughing beauty of a girl called Mary Lou . . .

I hate people who put dots after a paragraph. It sounds like they were practically swooning. Sometimes I think I am—and I guess you must think I am, perpetually, the way I laze around day after day without writing you, though I do think, "Golly, golly! If I don't write Mary Lou right off quick she'll be mad and she won't write me—get brisk, you big hulk; hurry!"

Then I come home, weary of juggling words all day long, of

piling phrase on phrase, of dipping into the punchbowl of language until I am dizzy, until words ring discord in my ears. I seize up a book—Galsworthy's "The Dark Flower" or Jane Austen's "Pride and Prejudice" or de Maupassant's "Boule de Suif" or the first great fat volume of "These Eventful Years" or Thomas Carlyle's "French Revolution"—and the evening is gone. Lights out. "I must write Mary Lou," I think, and think a lot of things, and drift off to sleep. It is ever so sweetly pleasant to drift off to sleep with my mind 3000 miles away, trying to picture what you are doing at that moment (five hours earlier than London time) and what you are saying and how your voice sounds when you are saying these things (which I make up). Now you are back from riding—a fierce, wild ride easing to a soft canter, gently caressing the hot smooth neck of your mount, bending low in the saddle and laughing; then away at the gallop again, faster this time and faster, with the blood pounding in your ears and a wild pagan zest in your heart—and home, cheeks flushed, eyes bright, a little slow-trickling wound in the heart that life is not all bending low in the saddle and laughing.

My boots are home in California. I am slightly insane about riding—the hot steam of heaving flanks, the triumphant bellow of this strong beast hugged and straining between my knees, the leap and the dizzy spinning reel of the canyon trail below: we had such lovely cool rides in the canyons there near Santa Monica, up around Will Rogers' ranch and Topanga canyon; I remember once I was so ashamed: I was riding with a party of sons of the sons of the old California dons, who knew how to ride, very gay in my clean white britches, and a brook came along, and I leaned, very gay to pick a flower off the bank—and suddenly, dismayingly, with no notion at all how it happened, I was plunked in the brook and scrambling out all dripping and muddy and miserable, and I remember a girl's silver-ringing laughter. Somehow, I have never felt about her as Heinrich Heine felt about the girl of his poem "In Meinen Tagestraumen":

In all my dreams by daylight
  And nights that follow after,
My spirit throbs and rings with
  Your long and lovely laughter.

Remember Montmorency?
　The ass you dared not straddle?
And how, into the thistles,
　You fell from that high saddle?

The donkey stood there browsing
　Upon the thorns thereafter—
Always will I remember
　Your long and lovely laughter.

But—I must make haste to answer your letter, or you will give me hell in the next. And I'm sorry, which is a stupid, inane word for expressing something you really mean, that my last letter didn't reply to some of your questions; but, honestly, Mary Lou, I guess I get so damn excited about my own thoughts of you that other people and things don't seem to matter. There are so many rushing, tumultuous things to say about you, and if I seem to go into hysterical lyrics about you, please just pretend it's silly or something. So anyway—before I make haste to answer that letter—I just want to slap you in my boots and wonder what the hell great inner bobblings you would get, if you were a man, if you were at college and a northerner, and it suddenly turned out that a girl you had never seen before was coming up for the frosh prom from a place romantically called Bluefield, West Virginia, but "Oh, good God! I bet she's horrible, fat and bouncy" and "Oh, of course, delighted to have her if she's a sister of that grand guy, Frank Archer"—said with agony—and then to see this dreaded "horrible, fat and bouncy" person step down on slim, enchanting ankles (Confession: I think I did look at your ankles first) and while you were still groping through the mist at seeing this trim grey traveling suit and then a lovely white throat and good chin—and everything!—while you were still groping, this softly enchanting voice said, "Hello, Roge!" just as though you weren't a poor worm standing there gaping stupidly at her—if you had seen that, Mary Lou, maybe you'd know how I felt. Now, ten years later, I find a snapshot, taken of you on a Nevada dude-ranch, somehow turning up in every pocket in my suit; and I . . . am . . slowly . . . going . . . daffy . . .
　So—

Be with me, Beauty, for the fire is dying;
  My dog and I are old, too old for roving.
Man, whose young passion sets the spindrift flying,
  Is soon too lame to march, too cold for loving.

I take the book and gather to the fire,
  Turning old yellow leaves; minute by minute
The clock ticks to my heart. A withered wire
  Moves a thin ghost of music in the spinet.

I cannot sail your seas, I cannot wander
  Your cornland, nor your hill-land, nor your valleys
Ever again, nor share the battle yonder
  Where the young knight the broken squadron rallies.

Only stay quiet while my mind remembers
  The beauty of fire from the beauty of embers.

I like that—by John Mansfield, Poet Laureate of England, who once swabbed floors in a New York saloon.

Page 3, and all I have done is meander. I turn back to the long grand letter on yellow paper, dated September 27, and I am afraid you have conjured up a fantastic picture of me as a glamorous foreign correspondent. The life here is a bit more sparkling than in New York or San Francisco, chiefly because it is abroad; but we work almost savagely hard, each one battling to make a name for himself in his three-year stay abroad, trying to gather fame as a Foreign Correspondent (in capital letters) so that he may go home as a Big Shot—"Oh, yes, I was a Foreign Correspondent in London, don't you know"—studying hard at history, getting a fairly intelligent and intelligible grasp on foreign affairs and international relations; re-reading Dickens and Thackeray and Smollet; plugging hard, almost like college again except that there is a bigger driving-force behind you; toiling by day, eight hours, six days a week, as you used to toil as a kid reporter on the New York Herald Tribune or the San Francisco Call-Bulletin; feeling smugly, "I'm a big foreign correspondent now," feeling, too, a little thrill about it—and wondering, "What will I amount to ten years from now?" A bleak thing to think about, Mary Lou, but

55

you can't help thinking sometimes.

I could draw you the brilliantly adventurous side of it—the spell of London; the bony, teeth-out-front English women who "quite adore Americans"; the nerve-racking jitters you get from sitting on the Cable Desk and writing flash-bulletins to New York on all the big news breaking all over Europe; the bobbing off to Scotland or Ireland or somewhere else on the trail of news, and a myriad other slants of this game. But that's newspaper stuff, for, to be honest, I should tell you, too, of the "famous European correspondents" from Iowa and Nebraska and Maun Chauk, Penn., with their babbity wives, all forlorn and pining to go home once more, fed to the gills with the "glamor" of foreign service and aching for a sight of the U.S.A. Personally, I love it, I'm dippy about it, and if I go home in ten years it will be too soon. I suppose it's because I've never had a real home town, because I've wandered all over the American scene, from Moosehead Lake, Maine, to New Orleans, from Seattle to Boston, and right now I'm finding England the enchanting "over the hill pasture" all animals seek.

I'm glad you liked California, Mary Lou. Of all the lovely places in the world to die, I think I would like to die there best of all—with the warm sun beating down, with the air sparkling clear and somehow sweet, and the waves booming up to the beach in my beloved Santa Monica. I want to live there again, and then die, with the white arms of the beach gently embracing the bay, gently embracing the soft breathing breast of the bay—for there, if I ever had a heart, I have left it. Yes, I am glad you like California.

Reno is funny, isn't it? You must have been heading west at about the same time I was going east, for I passed through Reno along about 4:30 A.M., November 4, 1934, driving, and barged into several chromium-plated bars where bewhiskered barkeeps were still pouring out villainous whiskey to rather wilted and chalk-faced gals from New York and points east. It seemed to me a fabulous combination of cow-town and Broadway, New York, with the cowhands falteringly trying to keep awake to entertain their eastern paying-guests. That was just a glimpse, though, at 4:30 A.M., sulky and tired.

I'd like to see young Mary Lou and Tempie. I get sort of ga-ga about kids; they do something to me I don't understand; they are the only thing that could convince me that married life, so far as I've seen it, is worthwhile. They make me notoriously sentimental, so much so that husbands among my friends regard me with pitying eyes, and laying their hands on my shoulders, say sadly: "My boy, too much meat has unhinged your reason." But I don't care; all I know is that they are so marvelously helpless and happy it almost hurts. I'm 31 now, and if, by 1939, I'm not married, I'm going to adopt a child to grow up with.

No, Mary Lou, somehow I can't quite picture you as a stenog or private secretary. The dashing young matron, whirl of social life and Junior League work, the gay and gorgeous days in Richmond: that is Mary Lou to me; and although I think you'd make a damn smart secretary, you don't seem to belong to the world of cold hard business. Please don't imagine I envision you as a starry-eyed innocent in crinoline, raising fluttering hands of bewilderment at such crass things as net profits and accounts. But what I mean is that bass rumblings of "Miss Archer—take a letter, please!" from a dyspeptic vice-president would probably turn out to be a lot less romantic than it sounds.

God knows, though, he might be a handsome dog.

FLASH: London, Nov. 24 (AP).—. A mad young American, waving a blue envelope post-marked "Bluefield, West Va.," struck terror tonight into pedestrians along the Strand. He was obviously demented. Questioned by police at Bow-street Station, he cried something about "a letter from back home" and burst into song.

It was sweet, and sweeter than that, to get your new letter today, Mary Lou. I left this letter unfinished last night, and then went to the office and found another exciting blue envelope in my box—and I began to believe in miracles. You are nice, Mary Lou, to write me in between times and not wait for the return letter, which takes so maddeningly long, and I will write oftener, too. The boats are slow. This won't go out for two days, and I guess by the time it reaches you it will be December, and then it will take almost ten days for any letter from you to reach me—or maybe, by that time, you'll have given me up as a total loss. I'd better cable you quick.

Of a surety, "the girl here" and "the man in England" offers a complicating plot—with the denouement on the lap of the gods.

Or possibly on the lap of Virginia Beach, Va. Nothing is impossible. I like to think that, at least, for your invitation is vastly alluring and I can think of nothing more glorious than basking in your radiance—oh, I know it looks silly in cold type: "basking in your radiance," but there it is—on this beach Down South. There isn't a prayer, really; I only get two weeks vacation: hardly time to cross the Atlantic and back again, let alone being too desperately poor to finance such a junket. I guess I'll have to stick to my original plan of going to Austria or the south coast of Spain—and only dream of you away off there in Virginia Beach.

Still, it might conceivably happen. I might be brought home, to New York. I might sell an article to the Saturday Evening Post I'm working on now. God knows what may happen in my funny, unexpected life.

Please send more pictures, Mary Lou. I love the one in chaps and ten-gallon hat—you look pretty tantalizing, you know. You've got a smile that wraps me into knots, and I can't do a thing about it so far away. The "thinker" is missing, can't find it anywhere. Tomorrow I'll stroll along the Thames Embankment and have one of those two-minute photogs do his worst, God help me! You're bound to be disappointed. I know I am, every morning mirror. I've had two urgent proposals of marriage since I've been here, the latest from the daughter of the governor of Penang, very old family, snooty, and all that; but it doesn't mean a thing in England, because they've got two million more girls than men, and my men friends tell me there is nothing to be either elated or alarmed about having the girl next to you at dinner suggest:

"Would you care to marry me tonight?"

And when you falter, bewildered, they simply shrug: "Oh, well, I thought not. But I just thought I'd ask."

It certainly makes things chummy, except that I do not care much or at all for English women. They are either disturbingly horsy, so much so that you momentarily expect them to neigh shrilly, or they look like a lost piece in a jig-saw puzzle. The daughter of the governor of Penang is neither: she is charmingly tragic and is a doctor of medicine with the funny nickname of "Players," and she is like a character out of Phillip

58

Gibbs' novels of the "lost generation" of post-war England. She drags me to ballets and to De Hem's Oyster House—I, who like neither ballet nor oysters. We quarrel savagely. On almost any topic.

It saddens but does not surprise me that your local papers don't carry the Greene by-line. When Mother was in Syracuse, N.Y., visiting my two brothers, she said she never saw my name on a story although the papers carried lots of AP London stories, unsigned; and at the same time, my Iron Duke was sending me clippings of by-lined stories in Oakland, California, and Portland, Ore. Lots of editors knock them off. We only get the Washington Post and the Baltimore Sun over here, and I've yet to see an AP by-line except for Jim Mills down covering the war in Abyssinia. There are 1350 AP papers, and I suppose about 300 of them knock off by-lines, with the old-time editor's idea that it's the story, not the name, that counts. Enclosed is a proof-sheet from New York to show you I'm still turning out pieces for the papers, however.

I've got to troop off to bed now, Mary Lou—very tired, utterly happy in the possession of your letter. And so,

With love,

Roge

New address: #20 Tudor Street, London, E. C. 4.

ᕬᔆ ᔆᕬ

Besides writing to Roge and writing in my journal, I kept track of my life with scrapbooks. I would sit on the floor in the middle of an enormous spread of photographs, newspaper clippings, and mementos. With the mind of a puzzle master, I glued each piece into place. I could see at least where I had been.

The process was messy and time-consuming, and I knew there had to be a better way. I had an idea for something simpler and faster—a plastic page or pocket that photos could be slipped into easily.

I thought the plastic page would be a good business venture and explored the manufacturing and marketing aspects of my idea. I made a research trip to New York and saw my sea captain, Harry Manning, who was in touch and wanted to finance the project, as

59

did others. I got a working model of my invention and showed it to people. Their response was enthusiastic.

Though it was feasible to manufacture, a lot of start-up capital was needed. I could get the money, but I realized that to make a profit I needed the sole right to manufacture my invention for a certain period of time.

A lawyer friend took my working model to the patent office in Washington. Unfortunately, it was deemed "not patentable," and I gave up on the idea. I did not want to invest other people's money without the assurance of a patent. I should have been more bold, but I could not take another risk.

I turned 29 that December and spent another Christmas in my childhood home with my children. Their father had remarried shortly after our divorce, and we saw nothing of him. He had a new marriage and new interests and was moving ahead with his life. I wanted my life to move on and was anxious about it. I was not the kind to sit around and brood, but I often felt stuck following my parents' advice, following my children, following because I was not leading.

Being both daughter and mother under one roof was tough. Sometimes it was hard to be home after essentially being away from home since the age of twelve. And Bluefield seemed dull after living in Paris, New York, and even Richmond. I wanted to travel, to escape, and occasionally to "run away from it all."

But the Christmas dreams of Mary Lou and Tempie were bright and dispelled my bouts with loneliness. I was glad 1935 was coming to a close.

✿✿ ✿✿

20 Tudor Street
London, E.C.4. December 20, 1935

Dearest Mary Lou:

Your letter from New York: very sweet. Yes, faintly I remember the nocturnal junket to Trenton and stopping the milk wagon and the crowded old car. Vividly, I remember the gay burning thrill of your laughter and the way a curl blew teasingly around a small lovely ear—and the dizzy madness of being near you. A long time ago in a place called Princeton and a girl I have never seen since, except in dreams . . .

I am envious of you, having cocktails in the Rainbow Room atop Radio City (I have never seen it) and having a grand time at the hockey match: you would be pretty gorgeous, I imagine, at a hockey match, with excitement-touched cheeks and dancing eyes and a lot of down-South cries which I wouldn't be able to understand at all but which would sound ever so warming nonetheless. The year after I went to California, I darn near married a Southern gal from Georgia just because she reminded me of you the way she talked. Lois D. Foley was her name—"It's easy to remembuh, jus' think of the initials and think 'Little Damn Fool' an' that's me!" —and we wandered up Malibu Beach on Santa Monica bay under the moonlight, and it was a strong moon, too, but the words stuck on an old memory, I guess, and she went back and married another Princeton fella who sent me their wedding announcement and said he was a class-mate at college, but I didn't remember him and anyway it didn't seem to matter. That was almost the last time I almost got married; there were some heady, tantalizing moments, but it was always no dice, and I have watched one after another marry off and dandled their kids on my knee while they beamed something about "say goodnight to Uncle Roger!"—and life went on. I'm a restless, self-centered cuss; I've always had a driving, dominant desire to be famous, and the curse of it has saddled me with an almost unconquerable feeling that I must be free to take chances, to go to hell and beyond, if that's where fame lies. It has certainly sent me scurrying around the terrestrial premises, throwing up jobs, suffering needlessly, forever hunting the new "green pasture" over the hill. London seems to be the best pasture yet, just now, but already I'm smoldering inside to go to Russia, or Vienna, or Paris, or Berlin, or Madrid—and some day I'll go. Do you know Don Blanding's poem:

There is a place I want to go,
A place called Parimaribo:
I don't know
And I don't care

61

Where it is
Or who lives there;
But just as sure as Fate I know
I'll go to Parimaribo.

There are so many Parimaribos; and as Toussaint L'Ouverture in "Black Majesty," said: "So much to do, so little time."

I have all your letters before me tonight, and I'll try to answer them but I can't swear it: I get to rambling off on wild goose trails before I know it, like that frightful long second paragraph on the last page. You say you're afraid I'd be disillusioned about the South and that it isn't half as romantic and glamorous as I think, but I don't know, Mary Lou, I've seen you and if that's the South I would be very fond of it indeed. I was appallingly disappointed, though, when I drove through there—Washington, D.C., Florida, Mississippi, Louisiana etc.—in 1931; it was early May, and I guess that explains it, but I went all bright-eyed expecting to see great plantations bursting with cotton and the Negroes plunking banjos and mournfully singing "Ole Black Joe" and there wasn't any cotton and the Negroes didn't have any banjos and they didn't sing and I felt pretty morbid and bitter about it. The next time I drive through the South I am going to take a phonograph with Bing Crosby singing "Way Down Upon the Sewanee River" which is the only thing he ever sang beautifully in his life, though God knows a million maidens stain their pillows with tears about him each night and this may sound like sheer blasphemy to you, too. Anyway, I did like the South, in my fleeting view of it: the bouilla-baisse and Creole dishes at Antoine's restaurant in the Vieux Carre, New Orleans, and the lovely old crumbling mansion houses. And I loved the sign on the privy door which bore the legend "Tinkle Parlor." What a land!

You say I should be writing a novel and that you have been expecting it for years. So have I. Even at Andover, fifteen years ago, before I got out of knee breeches, I was expecting a novel—just about like a woman expects a baby. I could feel it stirring in me and I would figure, "Well, it'll come any time now" but so far it has been a false alarm although lately I detect pretty positive signs that it's going to be real this time—even though it may be only a cerebral hemorrhage.

You still haven't sent me those pictures of young Mary Lou and Tempie; Good Lord, it's hard to imagine you all more or less grown up and the mother of two children, but it must be splendid, at that, and I often wish I had a couple of youngsters to kid around with. They make me pretty dippy; I go all soft about kids; they make me so damn happy to be with, they're so completely honest and friendly and they don't expect you to say something clever all the time or even any time. I'm supposed to be a "sparkling" conversationalist, but I hate it, I get stubborn moods when I simply won't say anything, which is, I know, childish; but conversation seems so cruel, to me: all the time you are trying so desperately to amuse someone whose own mind is about 75 percent involved in thinking up what to say next. The only people I like to talk to are children (under ten) or pretty women. There is something about a pretty woman that invigorates me; either that or strikes me numb. You can never tell about women. As Nietzsche says: "You can never tell about a pretty woman where the angel ends and the Devil begins." God knows why Nietzsche or any other man would want to tell, or be told: that's what makes life exciting and makes a mockery of the words in Ecclesiastes: "The thing that hath been, it is that which shall be; and that which is done is that which shall be done: and there is no new thing under the sun." Except, it should have been added, women.

I am reading the Bible, irreligiously but devotedly, now. There is so much marvelous beauty in it that it sort of thrills you—the simple, lovely beauty of it. It is too bad some of these goddam lazy preachers, if you follow me, don't gather their fuzzy wits and cut out all the bilious chaff, the boring repetitions, and finally present the Bible as a readable book, naked of dullness and empty phrases as Jesus Christ was naked in a manger in Bethlehem when the Three Wise Men came out of the East 1935 years ago. So I like the story of David's son, Absalom, and the climax—the most poignant cry in history from a father's heart: When Absalom organized a revolt and King David gave orders that under no circumstances was the boy to be killed, but a professional soldier killed him, and David cried out: "O my son Absalom, my son, my son Absalom! Would God I had died for thee, O Absalom, my son, my son!" —bending over the white cold body.

Nobody reads the Bible any more. Nobody goes to church any more. Personally, I'm a heathen, a pagan, a complete agnostic. But I hate to see beauty wasted, and the preachers are wasting it shamefully today because they are too bound up in their clerical collars and they have not yet found the happy medium between presenting the Bible either in the role of a stern disciplinarian or a hell-roaring Aimee Semple MacPherson or Billy Sunday.

From all this, you may gather the notion that I'm on the ragged edge of hitting the sawdust trail. I'm not. It's just an idea; I don't and never did believe in God, except one time when the Rev. Brewer Eddy got up on a Sunday vespers in chapel at Andover, when I was 14, and his voice was so lovely and his beard so white and long and splendid that I would have swapped God for him and tossed in my jack-knife and a gilded-framed photo of Mary Pickford to boot. But I wouldn't have given up my Oliver typewriter, which weighed 68 pounds and cost $75 dollars, for both God and the Rev. Brewer Eddy together, no matter how much the Rev. Brewer Eddy scared me and made me pray, shivering in my pajamas by my bed in the icy little room at No. 2 Phillips Hall, for mercy because I had just smoked a forbidden cigaret up the chimney. I was a funny little kid then, so pathetically earnest, trying so terribly hard, wanting so much to be liked; finally winning—and then when I did become one of the "big men" of the school, losing face with my peers because I didn't preserve the proper haughty, snobby manner towards the many unknown "punks" who didn't make frats and didn't become "big men" but were my friends. In all my life, there is nothing I'm more proud of than the vote in the Phillips Andover Academy Potpourri, the year-book, of 1923, which came from those "ugly ducklings" denoting me as the "least appreciated" man of the class. I guess, Mary Lou, I'm a "goddam Communist," as a young Randolph Churchill, son of Winston Churchill, told me one night at dinner. There is very little sympathy in me for the aristocrats; I come from a long, long stock of so-called "big wigs," among them my great-and-a-few-more-greats grandfather General Nathanael Greene on one side and on the other side John Paul Jones; but the little down-trodden guy gets my vote every time. I don't mean that I like to rub shoulders with the ditch-digger or the bar-maid; their minds hold nothing but human experience, which they cannot put into words. But that's just the point: they have never been given a decent chance, they've been ground under—and, in my simple idealistic soul, I'd like to see these humbler, embruted souls given the equal chance of "life, liberty and the pursuit of happiness" that we Americans boast about so much but only emblazon in a single line in a comic magazine titled "Life."

My Lord! what a paragraph! I go wandering down the lanes of wordage with all the blithe heedlessness of a child at a county fair.

> I am fevered with the sunset,
> I am fretful with the bay,
> For the wander-thirst is on me
> And my soul is in Cathay.

> There's a schooner in the offing
> With her topsails shot with fire
> And my heart has gone aboard her
> For the Islands of Desire!

Dick Allen, an old Andover school-mate, writes me that from California and says he has a yacht rolling in Santa Monica harbor waiting to take us scudding down the Pacific, with the spray singing against the bow, away and away down to the islands in the South Seas where there is hot sun and red-glowing sunsets instead of the cold grey fog of London—and the trim white craft is lying there in the harbor, the waves chuckling against its sides, and I cannot go. I cannot go. Two, three or four years ago—yes. But now I've got this career to carve out, for better or for worse, in sickness or in death. But Dick is waiting there, brown, hard-ribbed, laughing at life, on the white sands of Santa Monica bay, and how shall I answer him? You tell me, Mary Lou.

This business of living is so darn complex. If a human being could go alone, puzzling his own way through life, without friends, without interference, without temptations, it would be splendidly easy. But you can't! It seems to be forever the role of mankind to be "fevered with the sunset" and "fretful with the bay" and the wander-thirst is on them for their souls are in Cathay.

I want to chuck it. I want to go down to my office, to my fog-bound office, under the coal-smudged skies, in Tudor street, and say: "I'm quitting. So long, I'm fevered with the sunset and I'm fretful with the bay, and do you know where I'm going? I'm going to get the hell out of London. I'm going as fast as I can go to California and the warm blazing sun and slide into tennis shoes and white duck trou and a great guy named Dick Allen and I are going to sail down to the South Seas, and goodbye!"

We wouldn't have any money. Dick has a yacht, but he hasn't any money. He has a peachy wife, but no money and a yacht. We'd have to eat fish and mussels and a few more fish and maybe a nice dish of mussels the next day, but it would be fun. It would be fun to sprawl on the deck and let the sun hit your belly and hear the captain (Dick) bawl out: "Man the tops'ls! A squall coming!" and you wouldn't know how to man the tops'ls at all but you'd try like hell before the squall hit you. There would be bad nights. There would be pitch-black nights when the wind shrieked and screamed and the whole world turned topsy-turvy and you prayed to a God you had never counted on much before; the dishes would slide off their racks with a terrifying crash, the coffee-pot would careen drunkenly off the stove, there would be sickening lurches of the boat rolling a lot more than half over, and I can see you and me clinging to each other now, the way people do, in the frail but almighty terror people have. Then again, the sea is smooth; silver rides on the long cool waves and the night air is soft: the dishes below are washed, the bunks made; a slender wake bubbles like mercury away behind; starlight drenches down and in the darkness, an old sad song drifts out of the silence:

"Ay, ay, ay-ay! Canta y no llores!"

A song of Mexico. Sing, and do not weep . . . I don't feel like writing any more. Not now. I hope your Christmas is happy and your New Year very lovely, Mary Lou.

Ever and anon,

Roge

Chapter 7

Before I go on with this short history, let me make a
general observation—the test of a first-rate intelligence
is the ability to hold two opposed ideas in the mind at
the same time, and still retain the ability to function.
One should, for example, be able to see that things are
hopeless and yet be determined to make them otherwise.

—F. Scott Fitzgerald

O r that two persons, separated by time and ocean, and both
being "fevered with the sunset and fretful with the bay,"
stay put and plod along, tending to obligations and the
impossibility of their letters.

Fitzgerald wrote his opinion in the early months of 1936. His
observation struck a chord with me although my situation was
not as profound as his pain. His autobiographical essay "The
Crack-Up" appeared in three issues of *Esquire* magazine. I read
them and admired Scott's words and candor because he knew
that "there are always those to whom self-revelation is
contemptible."

Things were not hopeless for me, only dreary at times, and I retained the belief which Scott had seemingly abandoned that "life was something you dominated if you were any good."

Those gray, introspective days of winter seemed longest when they were at their shortest, and I wanted my life to be full again—not full in the sense of things to do because there were always things to do with children around—but full in the sense of purpose and optimism.

I was amazed by how freely I wrote Roge these things, the wanderings of my mind if not my person, the vague notions of the soul. All of this written to someone whose countenance I could not remember completely. I was not satisfied with my memory of how he looked at Princeton, and I really wondered if I would have been able to pick him out of a crowd. I wanted him to send me a photograph.

Each letter from Roge was a news flash. I loved his behind-the-scenes descriptions of the London bureau of the Associated Press—the "nerve center" of news from Europe and beyond. Though I was flattered by Roge's thoughts of me, it was the vivid accounts of his work and the people and London that fascinated me. At least at first.

His letters poured in during January and February and mine crossed back to him on the *Normandie*, *Queen Mary*, or *Aquitania*, my postman's personal favorite.

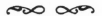

20 Tudor Street
London, E.C.4. January 6, 1936

Mary Lou dear:

Mad dreams seize me about you—and they have been stirring me, day and night, ever since your last letters. Tonight is the first chance I have had to put even a fragment of them down on paper, for I've just returned from a nightmare junket to Liverpool, across on the other side of England—covering the Lindbergh case.

As you may read about it in "Time" or "News Weekly," the story of the reporters' ordeal in covering Lindbergh's arrival may sound like exciting drama personified—and maybe, later, it will seem so to me on looking back. But right now it still seems an exhausting test of nerves. I didn't drink your warming toast "To Our Meeting in 1936" on New Year's Eve; I fell into bed at 7:30 and slept half an hour beyond the clock around, until 8 A.M., on January 1, 1936—tuckered out and dead to the world from 36 hours of cold, bleak work without a wink.

In the beginning: I arrived at Liverpool at 5:15 P.M. Sunday, along with some 50 "high-powered" American, British, and French correspondents and as many more cameramen. We hadn't the foggiest notion when Lindbergh's ship, the S.S. *American Importer*, would arrive. The steamship line itself had been sworn to secrecy, on penalty of being fired. I wirelessed the ship, and the answer came back, "No such person as Lindbergh on board." But we knew he was, because our New York office had cabled a confirmation that he was a passenger. We stayed up until 3 A.M. Monday morning, waiting for news of the ship; then back to the hotel to rest until 7 A.M., then back again to the pier—and we stayed there, in the chill-seeping fog, in the desolate dockland, with the foghorns crying mournfully until it got us all screaming-nerved, until Monday passed away and Monday night drifted into yellow Tuesday daylight and after a long, long while when it seemed that the human body really wouldn't stand for much more, the S.S. *Importer* crept out of the mist and stood off the Gladstone docks—and stood there for hours more before it finally slid through the canal to its dock. The boat docked, but still no sign of Lindbergh. We waited an hour; then suddenly, with baby John perched high on his shoulder, Lindbergh rushed down the gangplank, with cameras clicking and myself tearing for the nearest telephone booth to shoot the flash to New York, and then—the chase. I had my taxi pointed right, very fortunately. Lindbergh strode through the pier-shed, barred to all others, hopped in a waiting car, and came dashing out. We followed, self and cameraman. We had no notion in the world where he was going—our hunch was that he'd beat it down to Cardiff, in Wales, or up to J.P. Morgan's estate. My driver got caught on a red traffic light, and though I swore at him with every word at my command, alternately announcing that I would tear his jugular vein out and hang it on the nearest mistletoe and pleading with him that a traffic fine meant nothing compared to losing Lindbergh, he, with true British regard for the law, refused to go an inch until the green light came on. Well! I was fit to be strait-jacketed, but he picked up the trail again and under inspired urging made a rather beautiful run direct for the Lindbergh car—except that a carload of C.I.D. men (Scotland Yard) got itself interposed and we sheared off their fender very neatly and a big bruiser in the C.I.D. car slung a murderous look at us and started to get out and arrest us for probably treason on the high seas or God knows what, but anyway his car started off again with a jerk and he closed the door and that's the last I saw of him! So Lindbergh confused us all by going directly to the Adelphi hotel—right into the mare's nest where we "news-hawks" had been staying! And for three days, from Tuesday noon until Friday afternoon, he never put his nose out—kept his wife, Anne, and baby John, locked up there in that stuffy room while newspapermen representing almost every newspaper on earth tried to wangle a statement out of him as to why he had come to England—reportedly because he had been "driven out" of his native land by crime. You have probably read the stories there, about his having given the United States a "black eye" by leaving, and coming to this so-called "law-abiding" land of Britain. I don't believe he'd be such a fool as to make that statement. No man, of whatever nationality, ever renounces his own country: he's pretty damn proud of it, and he certainly wouldn't come to a strange, or at least a foreign land, and say, "I have given up my country. I never want to see it again." But that's what the N.Y. Times said he had said, and that's why some fifty odd British newspapermen had come down to see him: to try to get him to admit it, and to have him tell them that our America was a place where no man could live without fear, and that he had come to this "law-abiding" England to be safe. They are so infernally smug over here, and they were nonplussed, downcast and disgusted when Lindbergh wouldn't feed them things they could say to the glory of this prestige-conscious land called England to the detriment of America.

So anyway, Mary Lou, we had a fine time convincing these smug-ridden English reporters that no American, even Lindbergh, whose g—s no American reporter particularly admires, would give up his own country to come to this or any other land. They are too polite to break any noses, but in a more or less kindly way I intimated to them pretty thoroughly that Americans really are not sorry (contrary to the general belief in England) that we cut ourselves off from British tyranny a good many decades ago and that we are pretty damn pleased to be proud to be Americans!

I'm sorry, Mary Lou, to write such a five-foot paragraph; I won't do it again.

And so—

I turn again to your two letters, of December 7th and 18th, and my heart tumbles all around. They stab thrill-knives into me until I guess I'm just a romantic-eyed frosh at college again instead of a supposedly worldly foreign correspondent who has romanced with everything from Russian spies to hot-cheeked movie actresses from Hollywood to Elstree, England. I guess nothing I've ever known seems so important or splendid as Mary Lou Archer, 1924-1936.

Life takes you through queer tangled skeins. I think I have only had one steadfast ideal since time really began—and that was a lovely, glowing kid of a girl with blue eyes and a nose you thought about and tried to remember so hard long after and a silver-sweet accent that caught you somehow so that you didn't know whether to laugh or cry or what. I remembered your voice a long, long time . . . You were pretty glorious, Mary Lou.

But life beats a fierce tempo. And so it is strange to dream and drift over the words of your letter—and the miracle is there: it is just the same, the same handwriting, the same way you used to say things, until now suddenly it is yesterday and I come hurrying back from crew, gloriously tired after a hard spin miles and miles up and down Lake Carnegie, back through the soft spring darkness, to my mailbox in Nassau street to see if there is a letter from you before I go to Commons to supper. Tonight there is! I dash upstairs, four steps a leap, to my room and read it over and over again, and Bill, my brother, comes in and says, "C'mon, Roge, we're going to Trenton for dinner—some lads you'd better meet, upper classmen" and I don't want to meet upper classmen; I just want to stare out the window at the lovely spring evening with the trees all gloriously green and the skies rioting color and a song drifting from somewhere . . . and as darkness gathers down, I find my way to Commons where a ribald youth named Waltuh Hale jeers, "Boy, you better take some sulphur an' mo-lasses, quick! You look mighty pale!"

Spring-tide in Princeton. In England? I only know that even forlorn, fog-bound London seems a City of Enchantment when there is a letter from Bluefield, West Va., in my postbox.

Mary Lou, you mustn't think that this foreign correspondence game is always, by any means, a "fiercely tense and exciting life." It is more interesting than anything I've seen so far, but we simply work like anyone else at home—day after day, routine work, writing stories, not much excitement in a really big way; actually, it is entrancing to me, and I love it, the city, the life, the work; but it can't be much fun for the wives to sit at home, without many friends, until the big stiff of a "glamorous" foreign correspondent husband comes home to tell her what has been exciting in the day's work—just, I suppose, as the husband who is a broker or a banker or a vacuum-sweeper salesman comes home and bores the tears out of his wife telling her about the day at the office. And from all I've read, they are the bane of married life.

Over a long spell, it is, perhaps, glamorous. But God pity the wives of glamorous men. If you had been with me two weeks ago, sitting in the Distinguished Strangers Gallery in the House of Commons, on the historic day when Sir Samuel Hoare resigned because of the furor created by his Paris Peace Pact, you could have stretched out your hand and touched the Prince of Wales' golden head. Or this evening, you might have been with me at Ambassador Bingham's cocktail party at the American Embassy. But those are only high-lights between the long stretches of more or less routine.

I know only two wives who like it. They are Eleanor Driscoll, wife of Joe Driscoll, chief of the N.Y. Herald Tribune bureau in London, who adores her husband and drinks hard and would be happy in Hell; and Mary Sentner, wife of David P. Sentner, ace newspaper crime writer, of International News Service, and she'd get a great zest out of life anywhere. The others loathe it; they moan about getting back to their homes in Indiana or their little grey shacks in the West; and for all I know, they may be right.

Your letters are moonlight and magic, Mary Lou—and it is the devil, indeed, to wait. Your pictures cheer me, but it is a long way across the Atlantic and with my job here and mother living with me, it doesn't look very bright for my chances to hop over and see you at least this summer. Gloom engulfs me . . .

Well, honey, I am simply licked and must get this off on the mail boat in the morning. Please, please write me another long lovely letter very suddenly. It's an awful long time between boats.

With ever so much love, Mary Lou,

Roge

January 17, 1936

Mary Lou dear:

It is slowly beginning to dawn on me that Victor Herbert should have written, "Ah, sweet misery of love—at last I've found you . . ." Because, as your old Negro mammy may have told you when you were very young, "De misery's got me, honey chile" when I think of you and you so far, so far away.

Today, your letter cheered the gloom. Tomorrow? Well, tomorrow I shall read it once more—perhaps I can find new nuances, new undertones of hearts-across-the-sea in the four yellow pages that tell of your gay whirling life Down South. Then I shall turn to the blue pages of the letter before, and find dreams in them both, and even take solace from the fact that yellow and blue make—-. With a final "e," please. I am very fussy about that ultimate "e," for Greene is bad enough; Green would be simply unbearable. It reminds me so dreadfully of green grocers, with green apples and green cucumbers and, no doubt, mice. Sometimes, alone at night, I thank God that Gen. Nathanael Greene, the American founder of our family, had the decency to tack a final "e" on his name and so save us from the shame of being pointed out as having sprung from greengoods forbears. Now Archer is a fine heroic name: it smacks of keen-eyed, lithe-muscled men who pulled a bow for God, King and country in medieval days, and died gloriously. I had always thought Roger a sticky name until I came across it in the dictionary and found it meant, "Famous with the spear." I felt better about it then, and, aged about 9, used to thrust out my chest and say: "Ho, my lads! Follow me into battle, for I am Roger, famous with the spear!" It always chagrined me frightfully when one of my camp-followers would ask, blankly, "What battle?" It seemed to me a malicious trick of fate that there wasn't a battle raging around somewhere. I mean, you can't shake a home-made wooden spear and

73

shout,"Ho, my lads! Follow me into battle!" and just go charging off over the horizon wildly looking for a battle that doesn't exist and you know doesn't exist and so do your camp-followers. It may work the first time, and they may follow you until their tongues hang out. But after a while they begin to sulk and say they would rather play trains. Trains! when there is a battle to be fought, and dying men to kneel beside and hold their head in your arms, and then rise up once more and fling again into hot smoking battle! I had a good time when I was very young: the world seemed young then, too, and glorious. It has not changed, but I have. I have learned to think and judge things and be grave, without the child's joyous graveness, and I have lost the world of Make-Believe. Intelligence, it sometimes seems to me, is a tragic thing.

Perhaps that is why I love children. As Walt Whitman, in his "Leaves of Grass," wrote:

They do not sweat and whine about their condition;
They do not lie awake in the dark and weep for their sins;
They do not make me sick discussing their duty to God;
Not one is dissatisfied—not one is demented
With the mania of owning things;
Not one kneels to another, nor to his kind that
   lived thousands of years ago;
Not one is respectable or industrious over the whole earth.

A bad analogy, perhaps, Mary Lou, since Walt Whitman was not talking about children; but he was talking, per contra, against all the dark tumult of mature life. And, if you will read it over, you will see that it does apply to children—all except for the heathen penultimate line. For to me there is nothing quite so heart-stirring as a little child kneeling in prayer "to his kind that lived thousands of years ago."

My Christmas was gay on the surface, dreary within. It always is, without children. But your snapshot of Tempie and little Mary Lou, almost lost among their toys and the Christmas tree in the background, makes up for it. Tempie is adorable. She is the little one, isn't she? The picture of her standing in the snow in her galoshes, with that "Oh, well, dear me, if you must take my

74

picture—but do hurry, please, I've so many things to do" smile, is priceless. And then in the other, at the beach, laughing, pert little devil: "Hello, moms! Let's go swimmin'!"

Grand youngsters, Mary Lou.

I wish I could remember what I said to you about religion. Something pretty awful, I guess. But your paragraph, in return, is so splendid that I am glad if I did say something pretty awful. It is a straw to clutch to, when someone you admire so utterly does have a steadfast indomitable faith—and the strong heart to say so in this tinsel age when religion is almost sacrilegious to the tenets of pseudo-sophistication. In one paragraph, Mary Lou, you have hinted at some mysterious something I have always wanted to feel, but which always eluded me. Yet I wonder if this isn't what you mean by religion—the exaltation of having Tempie and Mary Lou so close to what are prosaically called heart-strings, the big-little day-by-day joys that swing life along pretty fine and free and dandy enough to outweigh fret and tedium, the glowing promise of tomorrow's unknown and enchanting morrow. In brief, happiness. And if that's what you do mean by religion, I'll worship it with you.

As for the rest—I don't know. I went through St. Paul's Cathedral today, through the crypt, and saw the tombs and plaques of Nelson, the Duke of Wellington, Lord Kitchener, and a glorified host of great men who were heroes in history but pretty grim martinets in life. I wonder not what they got out of it, but what their fellow-men got out of them: and I think the answer must be—a cold tongue, a stern look, a chill effulgence that compelled men to look up to them as though they were gods and not men. And last week I went to Westminster Abbey. The same thing. Kings, statesmen, naval and military heroes, and amid all their massive vaults and bronze and marble busts and plaques, on the stone floor, on a space not more than 12 inches wide, I saw these words: "O rare Ben Jonson"—and I think I would rather have that four-word cry written for my epitaph than all the flowery phrases, in English or Latin, carved on all the massive vaults and bronze and marble busts and plaques of the kings and statesmen of all time. In a roundabout way, what I am trying to say is that I would rather be simple and human, and maybe even kindly, than a cardinal or a king.

Well, I may be off to Russia soon. All very indefinite. But my Chief asked me how I'd like to go to Russia the other day, and I said, "I was ready—yesterday!" and he said, "Well, you might write a letter to that effect and I'll send it on to the head-office in New York." I have been slowly dying to go there for months. I'm holding my breath. I don't ever dare to think about it— except every other minute. It seems John Lloyd, the bureau chief in Moscow, has been out there almost three years, which is usually as long as they care to stay, and he'll be checking out for other points in a few months. So there may be a chance I'll get the post when he goes.

I don't know a word of Russian. But that doesn't seem to matter. They supply you with an interpreter, and not only that, but they give you a motorcar, house rent and servants in addition to regular salary.

Dreams, my dear Bolingbroke, dreams . . .

Right now, I'm studying up on my French, furiously. I'd had about eight years, private tutor in childhood, then at prep school and college; but when I hired a young Frenchman, three weeks ago, to come and teach me conversational French, very advanced, I found I was so darn rusty it was a shambles. He is very poor, and so he is coming to live in the apartment next week and exchange French for room and board. As soon as I can talk as fast as he does, I'm going to renew my nodding acquaintance with Spanish, which I loved more than any other language in the year I had of it at Princeton.

Two ayem. And so to bed, Mary Lou.

Hasta Luego, y con mucho amore,
mia carissima, my dear
Roge

January 31, 1936

Dearest Mary Lou:

These are furious days. This week:

MONDAY: spent batting the keys, madly, on advance stories about tomorrow's funeral procession for King George. A myriad angles. Six kings attending. Scotland Yard on guard to protect them against the possibility of stray "pineapples" from would-be assassins. The tens of thousands queuing up around Westminster Hall, standing hour after hour in the fog and rain and cold, waiting their turn to pass by the bier of the dead King. Yes, the day went fast. It was six P.M. (my quitting hour) long before I glanced up at the clock and saw that it was after eight.

TUESDAY: funeral day. I got up at 6:30, read the papers and at 8:15 sallied forth to cover the "crowd angle" of the gorgeous procession. By subway to Edgeware Road, just beyond Marble Arch. The whole town strangely alive, rushing, running, bumping, hurrying to a place along the route. The subway jammed—so crowded you could not breathe. Women beginning to faint. The guard cries, "All out!" at Marble Arch. All out here, or be carried on a dozen miles to the outskirts of London. "Why?" I asked the guard. "I wanted to go to the next station—Edgeware Road?" He didn't smile; he was already limp. "If you don't get out here, in a hurry," he said, "you'll never get out. The crowds are so dense they've choked up the exits to the subway stations." So I whizzed out and up onto the street level, hailed a taxi, and somehow he squirmed and edged his way through the mad-milling swarms of people to a place within three blocks of where I was going. I was going to Mrs. Dave Sentner's apartment, overlooking the procession route on Edgeware Road. I finally got through, elbowing my way in the good old American football spirit through what by now had become a mob as wild as Carlyle wrote about in his scenes of the French Revolution. Mrs. Sentner, wife of the International News Service (Hearst) star-man, had refused fifty guineas (about $260) for her front window. It was then about 9:45 A.M. Somebody shoved a tall tinkling highball in my hand, and although I never drink at that hour, I gulped it down with a prayer of thanks. The whole atmosphere was electric, super-charged with hysteria. I felt weak. The drink felt good. The others were already there: Joe Driscoll, London bureau chief of the New York Herald Tribune (my good friend from 1930-31 days when I worked on the H-Trib in New York with him); his wife; Newell Rogers of International News Service, and his wife; Mrs. Jack Bell, wife of another Herald Tribune man; von Faengl of the Chicago Tribune; Mrs. Darragh, wife of the bureau chief of the Chicago Tribune; an English actress named Wendy

77

something-or-other, blonde and tender; and one or two others whose names escape me at the moment. So we watched the massed crowds in the square below our window fainting, at the rate of two a minute, for two hours before the procession came into view with the coffin on a gun-carriage and all the kings, diplomats, soldiers, sailors, royalists and princes all in gorgeous uniforms slowly marching behind . . . a grand scene I will never forget . . . the people fainting like flies . . . we watched them through our opera or field glasses, and wagered on how many minutes they would take to recover before the next white-faced sagging body was yanked out of the swaying, surging crowd and laid down on a tarpaulin stretched on the gutter-side . . . and we pitied them, and I am afraid we (all Americans) were very rude on a funeral day of mourning because we drank highballs standing in the wide-open windows overlooking the scene . . . it seemed like a football day of a Big Game to us, and to them it was a day of mourning and intense emotion . . . something we couldn't feel, except partly . . . and they stared up at us, I don't know yet whether it was in envy at our lovely free-moving place to watch something that they had stood up all night long and all through the dawn and the morning to see, or whether they were staring coldly in disapprobation of our drinking and talking amid the solemn silence of their mass-hysteria grief. I don't know.

WEDNESDAY: a cold, fog-ridden day. Mourning over. Relief from the heavy city-wide suffocation of it lifted like a lung-smothering mustard plaster from the chest. I start to write a long, long article of about 6,000 words on the new king. Unfinished. Knock off, wearily, at six P.M., and after supper run out to Wembley Stadium, 45 minutes run from London, to cover a prize-fight between Jack Peterson and Len Harvey for the British Empire heavyweight championship. A photog's flash-bulb flares in front of me, but it is not until I see the papers next morning—

THURSDAY: that I find out it was a camera-chappie aiming in my direction, and that I am vaguely seen in the more or less immediate distance in a news-photo on the front pages of all the great London morning newspapers. A clipping is enclosed, with an arrow marking your correspondent, who seems to be thinking either about a blonde in the gallery or the paragraph of a story he is writing that he might have written better.

FRIDAY: That's today, or was until midnight shifted life suddenly into Saturday. Today I got up early: 7 A.M. My cherished friend, Ben Robertson, of South Carolina, whom I knew on the H-Trib when we were both pretty much cubs together in 1930 in the big-time newspaper racket, not a fellow AP-scribe, sailed this morning back to America, returning to Washington, D.C., so I put him on the boat-train at Waterloo station. He's been over here four months, filling in for a London staff-man who was sent down to Addis Ababa to cover the alleged war. Now the war seems to be simmering down, so Ben went back to help out in the forthcoming presidential election. After Waterloo, and so, as Samuel Pepys said, to work—writing a flock of yarns about this and that, and then home to play bridge until one A.M. with Dave and Mary Sentner and Mother: a corking game, hard-fought all the way, with only a sixpence changing hands at the end.

Well, Mary Lou, honey, that brings the diary up to the present minute, which is—2:55 A.M. The grate fire is glowing cherry red. The night is silent, except for the staccato beat of my typewriter. It seems lonely. I wish you were here. I wish you were here, sitting across from me on the soft-blue divan, so that I could talk to you about a lot things like shoes and ships and sealing-wax, and cabbages and kings, instead of knocking my fingers on keys that somehow won't translate the funny ache in my heart about you. Maybe you know Edna St. Vincent Millay's line about "Love like a burning city in the breast . . ." and maybe she was right. And maybe, too, you are only someone I dreamed about—and still dream on.

Climb out of the moon, my lad, and spin down . . . down . . . to earth.

So first—

The arrow in the newspaper-clipping photograph, as I said points to me. Another arrow, a long time ago, pointed the same way, only it was real—and that's why the white patch covers one eye. I was eight. After school, one day, we strung stout bows and whittled wooden arrows down to a splendid sharp point, and sallied forth into the woods to play Indian. My brother Bill stood fifty yards away and gave voice to a wild, blood-curdling war whoop, and stretched his bow. I peeped around the side of the tree where I had taken cover—and felt a shock. It didn't hurt much. I pulled the arrow out and the arrow-tip was red and I ran home a little scared and wondering why I suddenly couldn't see out of one eye but not crying, and then I stood in front of the mirror upstairs in the bathroom and saw what had happened and that's all I remember. But I remember I didn't cry, and I was pretty proud of that when all my little friends came to the hospital and talked to me in awkward, hushed tones and one of them told me I would be blind in that eye all my life—but I didn't believe it, not for a long time until Dr. Bentley took all the bandages off and I tried hard to see and couldn't see at all and then I began to tremble and I did cry hard because I was scared for the first time in my life.

I have never written or told this before, and it seems odd to do it now, because I have almost forgotten it for a long time. I'm supposed to look distinguished or romantic or something with the white patch, like Floyd Gibbons or Raoul Walsh, the movie director, and I don't mind it much any more.

So there it is. There's a fairly wide but close-clipped moustache, too, which wasn't there at the frosh prom at Princeton; but otherwise, I seem to be pretty much alarmingly the same, because I'd like so much to look grown-up and maybe dignified.

Dead to the world, Mary Lou. Please do write soon.

Your loving,

Roge

February 21, 1936

Dearest Mary Lou:

The days go fast. Life storms by. I struggle for balance, and tumble again into the spinning wheel. At times I long for sleepy California and the Land of Mañana once more; here it is not tomorrow, it is next week before you know it.

Today—February 21st. It stuns me, a little. Why! it was only yesterday I glanced at my mailbox and thrilled to see the familiar blue envelope, time-stamped 2 P.M., Feb. 1, sweet, and sweeter than that to write me: I love them more than I can tell you. Or vice versa.

Archer has been my favorite name for a long time. Good lord!

you do go back, don't you? Agincourt and 1400, and all that. And French, too. We must have just about the same blood count. I'm French-English, too, with a few spots of Scotch, Welsh and probably a little Pomeranian in me, as well. But my middle name, helas! is Denise, which caused me a good deal of mortal anguish when I was young because it sounded like a girl's name and a good many raucous noises like a horse whinnying or even a jackass braying, curdling my soul, would come from the lips of my gay companions screaming, for all the world to hear, "Hoo-hoo, Den-eeeeese!" I used to read gloomy tomes of black magic to learn adequately horrible curses to put on them. In a low, hollow voice which I fondly imagined rattled on a peculiarly darkling note, I would repeat: "Double, double, toil and trouble; fire burn and cauldron bubble. Eye of newt and toe of frog, wool of bat and tongue of dog—by the pricking of my thumbs, something wicked this way comes!" I always wanted to be called Bill or Frank, like my brothers, but instead they tacked on Roger and hammered it down with Denise, which is probably what drove me mad enough to become a newspaperman.

Nelson Eddy must have B. Crosby on the run. He's a new one, I think, since I came to this benighted land—and to illustrate how far they are behind the times over here, I just heard that piece about the music going around and 'round for the first time today, although I've read about it in American newspapers and magazines for months. Mother seems to have the same notion as you have, though; she saw him four times in Syracuse last summer, and was going to see him again when she suddenly decided to come abroad.

Well, they are still playing "Miss Otis Regrets" over here, or almost. Their music is pretty foul; the only decent radio programs heard in England are those from the French stations broadcasting American phonograph records!

Even the remote possibility of "you might find me in England sitting on your doorstep!!" isn't sufficiently punctuated with two exclamation marks. Talk about shivers of excitement! You want to bring me down with double pneumonia?

I wonder what would happen. I'd meet you at the boat, Southampton. I'd think, "Oh, my God, wouldn't it be too, too utterly terrifying if I don't even recognize her? Oh, Lord, please help me. I mean, Lord, it's a long time since Princeton and—"

And I'd stand there on the wharf and wave to the wrong girl and grin dry-mouthed, and then I'd see you with a funny kind of bobble in my throat and wave again furiously and probably break somebody's nose because I practically always have broken someone's nose every time I've waved in a crowd—it's just one of those little things that happens to everybody, I guess—and so after a while you'd come dancing down the gangplank just the way you came down the steps of the Pennsy railroad, and I wouldn't know what to do at all: whether to just act terribly calm and not at all flustered and say something about how I hoped you had not had a rough crossing and how were you and oh, I was fine, thank you, and pretend I was a Man of the World; or whether to just hug you tight and hold on and say nothing for a long time until my heart stopped jumping over the moon. I wouldn't know. I wouldn't know at all. I guess it would be better if I just found you sitting on the doorstep with the morning milk, because then I could say, "Well, my goodness, what a lovely dairy maid!"

"Sir!" she said.

"Yes, lovely," I said. "It is no use blushing, either. You know, you remind me vaguely of somebody."

"I do?"

"Yes."

"Am I supposed to be flattered?"

"Yes. You see, she was infinitely lovely. She was as priceless and radiant as the evening star, shining alone."

"Shall we dance, or would you rather smoke? You're smoking already."

"Be still! I remember the sound of her voice. It was a little like the soft, sweet tones of a carillon floating over the fields at dusk; and then again it was the gay sound of sleigh-bells singing across the snow on a bright winter's morn, and then—"

"You'd better lie down."

"Listen! And then it was husky and low, like Negroes singing away off somewhere, low and mournful—"

"You're hearing things."

"And all around, there was the scent of magnolia blossoms and jasmine, and honeysuckle in the hot sun—"

"This is serious."

"It is. Listen! She had blue eyes, sort of blue-grey, I think, that reminded you of nothing in heaven or on earth because they were both heaven and earth. Do you know what I mean?"

"Do I know what you mean?"

"No, you couldn't. Nobody could."

"Oh, nobody could?"

"No. And her mouth—but don't get me started about her mouth."

"Get you started? I wish you'd stop."

"Her mouth did something crazy to me."

"I can see that."

"It was the way she moved her lips, I guess—"

"You must be good at guessing."

"Or the way she smiled. Yes! That's what it was—the way she smiled! It tore your heart out. It made you want to do something about it!"

"Well, did you?"

"No, I—"

"You didn't want your sassy face smacked, eh?"

"Quiet, please! I'm trying to tell you about this girl. Look, were you ever in love?"

"Oh, no!"

"No, I didn't suppose so."

"I'm hungry."

"You'd better come in, I suppose."

"Will there be sausages and crumpets?"

"No."

"Well, I'll come in, then. But be sure the sausages are nice and browned so that they crinkle."

"Say, wait a minute!"

"I can't. I'm afraid I'll crinkle, too."

"You're—?"

"Yes."

"MARY LOU!"

(Exeunt, shouting.)

Roll on back over, Shakespeare, and don't you fret. I used to think I could write dialogue, but this scene went all simply screwy because where I meant it to be pretty emotional it went all haywire. Out in California, when I was writing for the emotional pictures, they said I had a fine future in it on account of I could write dialogue, with a wayward twist to it, but they did not pay futures and since returning to the galleys of journalism I've just about lost the touch. In fact, it seems, at this point, that I'll wind up just another old newspaper hack. I'm supposed to have a fine future as a foreign correspondent; I've been told by my chief on the AP and by my old boss on Hearst's Universal Service, before I came to the AP, that whatever gods may be have consigned me more prospects of big things ahead in the foreign service than any man of my age they have known; and I'm intensely interested in my toil and proud of being a scribe abroad. But you see, I want to be a big-shot writer, not just a newspaperman, some day. Paul Gallico, who writes those grand newspaper and other stories in the SatEvePost and who is sports editor of the New York Daily News, dropped into our office today, and I was pretty pleased when the chief of our bureau, who thinks I can write and may some day be an author, sang out, "Come back here, I want you to meet Roger Greene!" I was the only man in the office he brought Gallico around to meet, and I am afraid I burst every button in my chest because of the way it was done, although God knows I have met enough authors in my time and I must say that one and all have seemed exceedingly dull and floundering, except for Louis Bromfield who was a grand young man and totally drunk.

You talk, Mary Lou, about the "whirl of the golden newspaper game" and it is a whirl, all right, but there is practically no gold in a material sense to speak of. Except for a few headline-hunters of great fame such as Floyd Gibbons, H.R. Knickerbocker, Karl von Wiegand, James A. Mills and a few others, we grub and grouse along on mere pittances. Prices here are terrific. I pay $90 a month for my flat, which is on a very good street, just around the corner from Westminster Abbey and Big Ben, with two bedrooms, a maid's room, bathroom, kitchen and drawing room, but I could get the same thing on Nob Hill, in San Francisco, for $55. Bus fares are cheap—2 cents to Charing Cross, from here, and 4 cents down to the office on Fleet-street. Movies are three shillings and sixpence (87 1/2 cents) for anything decent. Liquor is 12/6, or $3.12 1/2 a fifth. You can't get a reasonable dinner at a restaurant under $1.25 unless you go to Soho, which, however, has the best food. The income tax is $1.25 out of every $5 you earn, although thank heaven we Americans don't have to pay it; all we pay is our American income tax, the office paying our British tax. Motorcars are a tremendous luxury: they are taxed $4 per horsepower, and you pay 37 1/2 cents a gallon for "petrol." The SatEvePost costs 18 cents, and Luckies, Camels, Chesterfields and other American cigarettes cost 1/6 or 37 1/2 cents, English cigarettes costing one shilling or two-bits. I've gotten into the habit of smoking British "Players"; couldn't stand them at first, but now I can scarcely smoke an American cigarette, they're so strong.

As for the "whirl" part of it, I'll give you a brief resume of the past three days:

Or make it two days, Wednesday seems so long ago:

THURSDAY: Take 11:05 A.M. train to Crowborough, down in Sussex, to interview Denis Conan Doyle, son of Sir Arthur Conan Doyle, creator of "Sherlock Holmes"; his mother is dying; they claim they are "in touch" with Sir Arthur although he has been dead these five and one-half years. Most interesting talk. Then back to London. Hit a bowl of soup for lunch, hurrying back to the office. Take off my coat, start for my desk, when the Cable Desk Editor says: "Better put that coat back on, Roge." And he handed me a ticker-tape message which read: "Col. Lindbergh visiting House of Commons." Then 3:10 P.M. I grabbed a phone, called the Foreign Office, argued them into giving me a last-minute pass to the Commons gallery (all passes are usually taken up by that late hour), picked up the ticket at the Foreign Office, beat it down Whitehall to Commons, found Lindbergh had only stayed 15 minutes, questioned the gallery attendants, scrammed back to the office and had my story on the cable to New York at 3:50.

FRIDAY (today): Up at 5:45 A.M., bath, shave, grapefruit, cornflakes half gone when our office chauffeur hammered the bell to take me down to Newmarket, in Cambridgeshire, to write a feature yarn on William Woodward's "wonder horse" Omaha, winner of last year's Kentucky Derby. Back to London at 70 m.p.h., driving like a movie gangster: because an opposition photo service had sent out a motorcycle man to carry back their camera plates, and our photo man, who was with me, had to get his plates back to London just as fast or he would lose out on selling the pictures to the British newspapers. So we chased this motorcycle man at the dizziest pace I have traveled in some semesters, weaving in and out of traffic hell-for-leather, missing a dozen smashes by rather less than inches, but getting there. I wrote my story, dashed off a couple of mailers, and then Mother and I went to a movie up in Piccadilly Circus. I forgot to explain that the reason we left so early was because Omaha gets up early for his morning canter, and it is a two-hour run out to Newmarket. I left the office at 4, and it is now 2:30 A.M., and I think I'll go to bed.

But first—that paragraph of yours about my doing you lots of good and making you want to do things and keep up. Good Lord, honey! I'm the laziest man alive! It would be grand to have another lazy-bones around if only so I could remember what it was like when I used to sprawl on the sands, in the hot sun, all day long in a place called Santa Monica, Calif.

Lots of love,
Roge

February 29, 1936

Mary Lou dear:

For once, words fail me. I fumble around the tumult of wild sweet emotions stirred to leaping life by your letter, and try to find some single thought that will express it—even mildly. In my adolescent years, before I learned the Hemingway value of under-statement, I would have said, "My dear—oh, my dear . . ." over and over again; and maybe I haven't learned so much about how to write, or maybe writing hasn't so much to teach about how I feel, because that's what I want to say, over and over again.

I must tell you everything about it. The whole staff, long since, has known about your letters. You see, our mail is put in cubby-holes, marked "JOHNS," "NUTTER," "BRAMAN," "PETERSON," "LEIDING," "OLDFIELD," "ANDERSON," "GREENE" etc., for all the world to see when they come around the corner of the editorial room—and everyone can see what everyone else has in his box in the way of letters from home. So I have come in for some very fine extra-fresh razzberries about the blue envelope from "that heart-beat down in West Virginia," and when I come into the office and they have seen one of your letters in my box, a great chorus goes up: "There's a letter edged in blue waiting in your box for you! Hallelujah, boy be saved!" So today this raucous orchestration went up, and I took a bow and went to a far corner to read your letter alone and undisturbed. I got to page 2 when I became aware of a harsh sound of off-stage whispers, as follows:

NUTTER: I tell you, the boy is blushing.

PETERSON: No, no! It's too violent for a blush. It's a rash.

NUTTER: He looks so wistful.

PETERSON: Ah, love!

NUTTER: Is there no hope, doctor?

PETERSON: None.

NUTTER: Alas! Our man Greene, I knew him well.

PETERSON: Hark, he still breathes!

NUTTER: No, it's just a sigh—life expiring.

PETERSON: Then you don't think he'll live, doctor?

NUTTER: As a physician, my son, I can only tell you that the patient is nearing a crisis.

PETERSON: Have you felt his pulse?

NUTTER: I have. It almost tore my arm off.

This sort of thing went on, ad nauseam, until I pounced fuming glances at them and went clear over to the other side of the office to read on. You see, I'm the only bachelor in the office and they are taking it out on me to a fare-thee-well. They want to know when you are coming over, and do I think she'll marry me, and they slam a flock of molten questions at me which I have no intention of revealing to the press at this time.

"Later, gentlemen, please!" I tell them. "Have you no regard for the sanctity of the home?"

"None!" they shout.

"Then think of my wife and children," I beg. I mean, that's supposed to curdle even the heart of a hard-boiled newspaperman. I have had hundreds of people ask me to think of their wives and children, and I have thought of them without it helping at all to give me a lead for my story.

"Greene," they said, solemnly, "do you confess to all?"

"All?" I said.

"All," they said.

"You mean—all?"

"Yes. All God's chillun got wings. Let's dance!"

So that's the way newspapermen are, Mary Lou. They are pretty vicious. They have no feelings. They are cads. I've just been told all this two hours ago. It is now 1:30 A.M. At 11:15, the office called me. I had just arrived home from work and barely finished dinner. I felt pretty shot. I'd been up since 7 A.M. Mother and I went out to Richmond to play golf, and I turned in a 52-44-96, which is horrible but my first time out since last October, and anyway, after golf and a day of toil thereafter—interviewing Lady Ashley about whether she is going to marry Doug Fairbanks, and attending a cocktail party thereafter with Sir Malcolm Campbell and Lord Howe to be interviewed about their plans for new assaults on the world speed records—after those two jobs and batting out a "high-powered" cable story about the Jap revolt in Tokyo, I was ready for sleep. Then the office called. Barbara Hutton, after birthing a son, was allegedly more or less dying. So I hopped a cab up to her mansion at #2 Hyde Park Gardens to get the dope on it. Three English reporters were hanging outside the house. I asked them what they had. The said nothing; they were just waiting. I punched the doorbell and freakishly enough, Jimmy Donohue, Barbara Hutton's clown cousin, opened the door on his way out. So I told him: I said that our newspapers in America (some 1350 of them) were anxious about the condition of Barbara and that much as we appreciated their desire for privacy, it was a matter of legitimate news if the richest woman in the world were dying. I talked fast. Donohue said her condition was "very serious" and then froze up and put on the Lindbergh chill which has made every newspaperman in America hate him, and said a few things about "Good God, haven't you newspapermen any sense of feeling? Why do you pry into private things that don't concern you?"

I said: "All right. You're worried. Skip it."

He slammed the door, screaming something about reporters being rats. And maybe he's right. All I know is that New York cabled us to "upfollow Haugwitzess sharply soonest" and that meant every newspaper in America wanted to know if Barbara Hutton was going to die and that I was sent out to find out, and maybe it was prying to ask whether the heiress to $40,000,000

American dollars reaped from the American people by sweating American five-and-ten shopgirls was dying. Maybe it was wrong to ask, and maybe the whole system is wrong, and just possibly maybe again people who have gained the world limelight, either through ill-gotten gains or God-given genius, would be just a little more kindly and tolerant of other people's morbid curiosity as to their welfare and being.

I don't know. I only know that in 10 years of newspaperdom, the biggest people have been those who talked genially for publication at any length required, and the smallest people were those who either had something to hide of which they were ashamed or had an incongruous idea of their worth. I have, I think, talked to almost every type of human being, from Einstein down to the Brooklyn alcohol king, in prohibition days, who unhappily ran into a barrage of sawed-off shotgun slugs and had his hand sprayed clear off when he put it up to shield himself and a hole chopped out in his chest around the heart big enough to shove your fist into it without touching anything.

Well, it was funny. Donohue banged the door and about two minutes later, while I was talking to a couple of British journalists, he came slipping out a side servants-entrance. I had to hit a 'phone. The only way to a 'phone was down to Marble Arch, which was the way Donohue was going. He looked over his shoulder and saw me. He quickened his pace. He is a little guy. I am a large guy. My legs are long. I didn't want to embarrass him. But it was cold. I struck out at a good pace. Donohue knocked his pace a notch higher. I still was overtaking him, and he casting glances over his shoulder. Fifty yards ahead, he stopped by a lamp-post, beat his stick against the curb to show that he was annoyed at being "followed" and then went on. He strode ahead at a good clip. His legs are short. Mine long. I passed him. He looked at me. His jaw fell. He so obviously expected me to whirl on him and ask more questions. It was a little comic. I didn't even look at him in passing. I think he will never get over the disappointment of my sailing past when he thought he was being followed. You see, what is funny, Mary Lou, in retrospect, is that Jimmy Donohue fully believed he was one of God's greatest creatures from a newspaper standpoint at that moment, angrily ready to refuse an interview, trembling with outraged indignation, and my own brain vaguely remembering grand happy interviews with Bernard Shaw, George Arliss, Lord Snowden, Charlie Chaplin, Jimmy Walker, Franklin D. Roosevelt (when he was governor of Nyk) and a lot of human kindly people who didn't have a cousin worth $40,000,000 but who were very good to talk to.

Well, I don't suppose I should brood about such picayunishly irritating interludes with newspaper-haters like Barbara Hutton, Lindbergh and Lady Ashley. There are dark moments in every business, and on the whole this newspaper racket is pretty enchanting.

March 3, 1936

I seem to have gone dreaming off, above, with the intervening days very full. We had some people into dinner very late Saturday night, then Sunday night there was a large brannigan at Dave Sentner's which wound up still drinking champagne cocktails at 3 A.M., and last night I wilted into bed at an hour Benjamin Franklin would have beamed at. It is a pretty gay crowd here, among the expatriates of the American colony, and I guess I am just a country boy at heart because these late hours and fizz and other strong waters leave my tissues very limp. My head seems to be ticking along all right now, but all day Sunday I was pretty ghastly certain that somewhere in the mix-up I had mislaid my own head and brought home somebody else's: it was too big, it didn't fit at all, and it hurt.

I only hope that if your last letter is any criterion of how you write when you have "been working too hard and feel cross and lonely"—that whenever you feel the slightest symptom that way you will rush for the nearest pen and write me another. A grand letter, Mary Lou, and I only wish, too, that you were sailing today with your friends for that three-months trip abroad. Who knows, you might like it over here more than three-months worth.

It gives me a great glow—men are hopelessly vain—to read that you think I am "gallant and fine" and I'd like to be just those two words especially; but I'm afraid you'd be shockingly disappointed. It saddens me a good deal that I neither look like Ronald Coleman nor talk like Michael Arlen: that I am, in fact, as average dull a person, lazy, arrogant, shiftless, profligate, weak-willed and generally uninspired, as ever filled an idealistic-minded girl with disgust at the whole male of the species. I drink too much. I start endless short stories and novels—and they remain endless. I never do half the things I mean to do. I spend all my money and am broke, regularly, a week before pay-day. In fact, I'm an oaf and I just won't admit it.

I chuckled over your comment about my picture in the paper. Yes, I should be up more in the front next time. You see, what happened, of course, is that the photographer was taking a picture of me but all these people shot up at the last moment and got in front of me. Camera-hogs, my dear, just camera-hogs. So anyway I had our photo department get me a glossy print, a snip of which is enclosed. Sooner or later, I'll have a solo picture taken, although I am not eager to do it because I do not admire my pan at all and I would not care greatly to think that there is more than the original going around.

You say "we have so little that is tangible for either of us," and to me it is forlornly true. I cannot even say I miss you, because I have never had you except for one fleeting lovely weekend so long ago it is a sheer miracle it still seems so little a time ago. We have only written words, without sound of voice or sight of speaker, and I am more than a little afraid that where you might reasonably fall in love with my words, because it is my whole life to be more or less clever at marshaling words, arranging them in gay or sombre or heart-catching patterns, just as reasonably if not more so you might find it fantastically impossible to love the real every-day R. Denise Greene in the flesh as you thought you loved the RDG of the typewriter. It is a very sad thing, but I am too much a realist to believe that actual love can be platonic—a sort of suspended plane of mental reciprocity, so to speak. I am afraid that theory is all very pleasant for 80-year-old philosophers to tilt on their fingertips like multicolored bubbles; but it is the curious and paramount thing about bubbles that they do explode, and it is the similar thing about human nature that explodes and sends a boy and a girl, or a man and a woman, or even an 80-year-old philosopher and philosopheress, rushing into each other's arms that is really this funny thing called love. It is a troubled hunger for someone to cling to, alone and unmasked as against the eternal masquerade of life outside, that accounts for love.

All this, of course, is absurd. I've never been married. And how could you really know much about love until you've been married? I surrender. Yet I do know it's got to be tangible: only there's this queer thing that bothers me and smashes my ideas to smithereens—you're not tangible, and still when I go to these parties and meet pretty radiant girls, they leave me cold against the sirocco winds from a girl called Mary Lou 3000 miles away.

As to that, bonne chance. I see no prospect of going "home" for years. My whole future lies abroad, and since I have no particular home anywhere I have no great urge to live in the United States, whereas I have a boundless desire to become, some day, a famous foreign correspondent roving over the face of Europe— like old Jim Mills does now. Jim is the AP roving scribe; he has been down in Abyssinia covering the war, but now that the war is simmering down and the Far East situation is getting torrid, he has been ordered to progress leisurely through India, writing stories there as he goes, then on to Shanghai by mid-April and thence on into Manchukuo just in time to cover what now seems to be an impending Russo-Japanese war.

Wherever the news is breaking, Jim goes there. He has no home; he's a bachelor. He's in the thick of the world's great headlines year in and year out. There's not much comfort in a life like that, I suppose, but migod, it is living!

I've a long way to go. My boss tells me I'm a better, more graphic, more thrilling writer than Jim Mills. But I'm too darn young to get such an assignment, and I've only been with the AP a little over a year. It takes a long time to build up a reputation in newspaperdom: there's only that shining goal ahead. Sometimes, I wonder if I want it; I wonder if it wouldn't make a happier life, in the long run, if I stifled this restlessness, this wanderlust, you might call it, which has driven me from every job, from coast to coast and now to England, in quest of Lord knows what. But I seem to be built that way. I knew I was going to try to be a newspaperman when I was fourteen, when most of my friends hadn't even begun to think about what they wanted to do. I "heeled" the school newspaper my first year, and almost literally fought my way to be editor-in-chief two years later, and twice was almost kicked out of school because I wrote the news cold and raw instead of sugaring it or ignoring it. Once, Headmaster Al Stearns was livid about it. I wrote a "powerful piece" about the green-tainted eggs and foul food in the school "beanery," and Al got up in chapel and preached twenty-five minutes of Dantesque fury against this "most scurrilous attack on the fair name of Andover in the history of the school" and then called me up on the carpet and terrified me until I could only stammer out miserably, "But Mr. Stearns, sir, the eggs were green!" He said gruffly: "I was young once. Now, go back to your dormitory!"

3 A.M., dear. My coal fire at last has driven out the chill smoky fog, and the warmth of it and the lateness of the hour makes me fuzzy. So to bed. Please write soon.

Your adoring,
Roge

In my journal of *Thoughts*, there is a poem. In parentheses at the bottom, I put the name: (Roge Greene—1924) The words are not his, but there is something of Roge in the verse.

Across the fields of yesterday,
He sometimes comes to me.
A little lad just back from play,
The lad I used to be.
And yet he smiles so wistfully
Once he has crept within,
I wonder if he hopes to see
The man I might have been.

Chapter 8

M other wit is a phrase used in the South mostly, and one I have heard all my life. Some Southerners argue that you either possess it or you do not, that it cannot be learned. You are simply born with it.

To define it is difficult because it is a quality, an attitude, a grace. It is a sense of balance and of humor, with the scales tipped toward hope. At its finest, it is wisdom and knowledge of life's continuum. At its lowest, it is a shrug of the shoulders. It is often wry and witty, but always serious with hope as a mother should be.

Mother wit is moderation and excess is discouraged. Too much charm is false; too much humor is ridiculous. Too much despair is debilitating; too much woe is not fair.

As with all graces, it can be lost or covered up by life's misfortunes. But if you were born with it, as they say, you want it back when you discover its absence in your outlook. I recovered my mother wit during the spring of 1936.

Perhaps the warmer weather and promise of springtime undid my gloom, the sense of new life coming on after being stalled out by the sad but necessary choice of divorce and relocation.

That spring I began to feel better and saw that I was at a

point in my young life and not at a period at the end of it. I began getting out of the house without worrying about Tempie since her winter bouts with asthma seemed under control. I saw friends, went horseback riding and golfing, and played bridge and a new game called "Monopoly" that was a sensation.

April 20, 1936

Mary Lou dear:

I'm an oaf. A great oaf. An utter oaf. For three weeks now, while entertaining a visiting fireman—an old confrere from San Francisco—I've put off writing you "until tomorrow." Can you ever forgive me?

I'm hugely sorry, Mary Lou. It seemed to be one thing after another: something every night. Thank God, he sails tomorrow and I will try to make up for lost time henceforth.

Just at this point, it seems I may be back in New York in about four months. It's all a little complicated, but here's the dope:

I joined the AP here in London, before that having been a Hearst man. That was all right and no complaints from the Nyk head office, despite the fact that there is an old AP rule that all AP foreign correspondents must be sent abroad by the Nyk office and not hired over here. No objection was raised, however—in fact I've had highly complimentary letters on my work from the five top executive editors, including the Great White Father, General Manager Kent Cooper himself—until the London bureau chief, Frank King, asked Cooper for a fat raise for me. Then Cooper wrote back reminding my chief of the old AP ruling and saying that Nyk has a long waiting list of long-time AP men who have been waiting years for a chance to come abroad—and that if the chief thought I ought to draw a big salary worthy of a topnotch correspondent, he (Mr. Cooper) would send over a man already drawing a big salary from the Nyk office to take my place. Cooper is hard as nails about money, and apparently he forgot that in his bouquet letter to me he said he would "watch my career with interest."

So anyway, in order to get more money, I've got to go back to Nyk and let them look me over. I wanted to go at once: the sooner the better, since it has to be done. But King insisted that he can't spare me during the coming busy summer months; so it wound up by my agreeing to stay on here until early fall.

The whole thing is a bitter pill, in a way. I love it over here and believed I was carving out the foundations of a fairly sparkling career abroad. In the 15 months I've been on the AP, only one other man on our staff of twelve Americans has had a single letter of praise from the Nyk "powers that be"—and it seemed I was making good in a big way. The Chief thought so too, apparently, and tried to get my salary hoisted to big-time figures. But paradoxically, because of that, I've now not only got to wait more months before I get a raise but I have to give up this foreign career and go back to Nyk at least temporarily.

It is pretty infuriating . . .

And yet, maybe that's destiny. There must be some unseen hand that keeps jerking me, puppet like, back and forth and around and about the terrestrial premises—Cleveland, Seattle, Denver, Boston, Chicago, Princeton, Santa Monica, New York, San Francisco, London, and now New York again.

One BIG advantage—I'll be able to see you, if you haven't gone off the deep end about some soft-eyed Southerner by then. Maybe you would come up to New York, and we could barge over to Princeton to see the football games . . . or drive up through the lovely, golden countryside to visit my brothers in Syracuse and Lake Skeneateles . . . or even to 'Sconset, on Nantucket Island, which is something special with the rambling rose-covered old cottages and the song of the surf booming all night over the bluff and the clam-bakes and the salt tang of the sea and the lonely sound of the sea . . .

I love every line of your letters, Mary Lou—about the young ladies of old Virginia swooning at Nelson Eddy, and Ann Byrd in what might be called a high resolve not to take a bath for a week to preserve the Eddian oath written on her back. It is grand to roam with you in your jaunts around the countryside in the new Plymouth (pretty nice!) and it is very forlorn indeed when I do not hear from you. I read the old ones over and over again, chuckling all the time because your humor is simply exquisite particularly when you get all gloriously breathless and exclaim, "Really dear after all this I don't believe I have made one sensible statement—so skip it!! please." Believe me, you have; every word sparks electricity—oh, you are pretty extra splendid, my dear, and then some!

Lord, you have a gay time, too! If London sounds like a gay whirl to you, your life down there, dancing around from one place to another, sounds far headier than it is here. I went to Aintree, in the north of England, to cover the Grand National steeplechase late last month—four giddy days of watching the bang-tails and it was almost uncanny how every horse I bet on seemed to think he was chaperoning the rest of the horses and had to stay behind to see that none of them got lost, strayed or stolen coming into the homestretch. In one race, I went "all out," as the British say, and planked a few bob on the two red-hot favorites figuring one or the other would surely win, and I will be eternally switched if those two oat-burners did not finish flank-to-flank in the complete background.

So then, on Grand National day, I decided to recoup my ebbing fortunes, and I talked to Pete Bostwick, the American rider of Castle Irwell, and he said, "Confidentially, I like my chances very much." So I put a few quid on Castle Irwell— and as I explained in my cabled story of the race, "a quid doesn't mean a chew of tobacco in England. It means $5 each." Anyhow, this Castle Irwell was pretty much of an old ruin as far as I could see, and he came puffing home in seventh place shortly after sunset. I think I will stick to golf.

Had a lot of fun last night kidding around with Lupe Velez at a cocktail party in Mayfair, drinking "white ladies"—and how that Mexican pepper-pot can drink! She's a pretty nice kid, even if she does keep reminding you that she gets $3500 a week and fondles practically everything in trousers. There were a whole flock of English "dramuh" critics there, and just three of us American correspondents, and Lupe lost no time in letting the Britishers know that their company left her cold. One big English director came sidling up with a girl he wanted to introduce to Lupe, and La Velez merely nodded and then turned her back on them to resume a roaring argument we were having about her fights with her husband, Johnny Weismuller. She's a wildcat, all right.

Today I've just finished a series of articles on British and American crime which you may see in some of the AP papers early in May. So it goes. Some fun, a lot of hard work—and a dreary feeling when I don't hear from you, dear. I am so annoyed at myself for not writing sooner; I'll never do it again. I've discovered, in this interim of silence, that you mean just about everything to me.

Now long past midnight. Please, please write soon. No words can tell of—

My love for you,
Ever,
Roge

May 3, 1936
Sunday night, 1 A.M.

Dearest Mary Lou:

A roaring night. Apparently all hell broken out in Addis Ababa. Nyk yowling for copy—and the wireless station, at Addis, on the blink. So there is nothing to do but cable Nyk "NOTHING PRESENTLY AVAILABLE EXADDIS COMMUNICATION OFFCUT." But does that satisfy Nyk? It does not! They cable London right back, with your correspondent in charge of the news desk: "WATCH ALL WIRELESS STATIONS OFFICIAL UNOFFICIAL WHICH MAY CAPTURE ADDISABABA REPORTS STOP NEED COLORFUL HUMAN INTEREST TERROR SCENES STOP NOTIFY PARIS WATCH BORDEAUX RADIO ALSO SWISS NOTIFY ROME BERLIN."

So I 'phone Paris, Rome and Berlin, and meanwhile cable back informing the cuckoo and slightly hysterical Nyk editor that any wireless reports sent out from Addis Ababa which might be picked up by European stations would all be sent in code—so that it would be meaningless, gibberish even if they did pick it up. A lot of fun, though slightly hectic: because, you see, this was Saturday night and the usual full staff of my American

99

confreres was missing, so that I was left alone on the desk to handle everything, with only two cable-operators, two telegraph editors and an odd office boy or two. That may sound like a lot of help. But all they do is routine work; they do what you tell them, and that's all. Meanwhile, you, as the sole editor, have to handle the constant stream of copy from three news tickers; you have to scan the repeated new editions of the dozen-odd London morning newspapers to see if they have anything worth cabling; you have to edit all continental AP- bureaus copy which is 'phoned through London; you have to call them—Paris, Berlin, Rome, Madrid, Vienna, Moscow—and keep them informed of major news events, because London is the news-heart of the European world: what you might call the brain-center of the western world; and there are several thousand and one other details in handling the London office of this world's biggest news agency, believe thou me!

I was glad to knock off at 12 midnight, weary from work mentally, and weary physically from 18 rather deplorable holes of golf out at Richmond this morning before I took over the desk at 4:30 P.M. I had a 45-42-87, and I guess it is human nature that I shall not dream tonight about an 8-hour stretch of tumultuous toil at the office but about the shots I missed out at Richmond— the putt that licked the cup so heart-breakingly and did NOT go down, and the long curling iron-shot that curled, alas! too much, into the bunker. It may seem strange, but a bobbled drive or a shanked mashie-shot has a more profound emotional effect than a whole night of sensation-ripping news.

Period. Paragraph. About my business—and golf.

I think I have never been so confusedly happy, Mary Lou, as when one of the cable operators brought me your message of five words: "WHAT HAS BECOME OF YOU." I say confusedly because, as I tried to explain in my last letter, I felt mighty bad about the long delay in writing you and I was pretty continually worried that you would just forget all about me and not give a damn and wonder why you had ever bothered at all about me in the first place. And then—oh, and then!—Lord, I felt good that you would bother to cable: it seemed to mean that you liked me enough to skip the usual feminine retreat of wounded silence, and instead said just exactly what you meant. It thrilled me, and

I think you are pretty extra splendid, Mary Lou.

In answering, I cabled "UNHAPPILY NOTHING" because I seem to be getting restless lately and nothing much has happed really. My whole mind is on fire with a craving to do things, to have things happen to me, to be sent out on a big story, to be sent to Paris or Moscow or Shanghai—just to have something happen to me. I love London, but always there is that impelling desire to roar off somewhere else: meet new people, see new things. And I shall. I've got to! Right now, incidentally, there is an opening in the AP in Shanghai—and if I can only get Mr. Cooper, the General Manager, out of the idea that I should come back to New York, perhaps I'll get the chance. The only reason in the world I would want to go back to New York would be to see you, Mary Lou. Europe has got into my bones, and except for recurrent flickering twinges of home-sickness, I would almost want to stay over here forever.

I don't know what it is, exactly. Certainly I get morbid amid the gloom of London's perennial fog, and I long and long for the bright hot sun of California; I long for the white beach sands of Santa Monica and the blue clear sky above; I want, with a burning fever, to drive once again out Wilshire Boulevard from Los Angeles and stop off at the "White Spot" for a hamburger bun loaded with mustard and pickles and peppers and a faint trace of onion, and good cup of American coffee—and then race on to the Beach Club to dance until dawn with an honest-to-goodness American girl who won't act bored to tears but may even seem to enjoy herself. These dead-pan English girls look like an accident going somewhere to happen, and it is my notion that if you stuck a match down inside their shoe they would merely suggest that another window be opened. A burning match, I mean. Oh, they make love willingly: I don't mean they're cold that way. But they are as dead of any romantic fire as the grey, inanimate ashes of the morning grate. It is the English way, and all I know is that it turns an American man celibate.

I think I would have given anything if you had been here Thursday night—for the opening night of the Midnight Follies at the Dorchester in Mayfair. A grand party. Michael Arlen sat at the next table, just about touching my shoulder. Sandra Rambeau, former mistress of King Edward, was there. So was the Marquess of Donegall, and most celebrities in town, including my old friend Miriam Hopkins, very lovely, who is now a big-time movie star but was just beginning to blaze when I first met her, sitting next to her, with Joel McCrea on the other side, at a Sunday morning sausage-and-waffles party at Frank Dazey's house in Santa Monica four years ago. I dropped over to her table and spoke to her, wondering if she would remember me, and I guess I was pretty pleased when she did remember and started talking old home town.

The party was all "on the cuff" for our table of American newspaper correspondents—Dave Sentner of International News Service and his wife, Tommy Watson of Universal Service and his frau, myself and a blonde. Our bill was 15 lbs, 13 shillings, or $78.25 for the six, but naturally we didn't have to pay for it. Everybody else drank champagne; I stuck to a cool, unsparkling dry French wine—Piesporter '27—because champagne darn near cracks my head open.

But what I started to tell you was that I dragged an English blonde—oh, nice and attentive—but when I was dancing with her or talking to her at the table I was sadly conscious that neither she nor anyone else would do, at all, and that I missed you . . . missed you . . . missed you . . .

I don't profess to know how you can miss anyone when you have only seen them for one brief week-end, but I guess Tin Pan Alley had a pretty good idea on the idea that "love is a funny thing—it is the strangest thing . . ."

Nothing further, so far, about my going to New York. That's the way things work in the AP. You're in a groove, and don't know what is going to happen next. Then you get a cable, and the next day you're on a boat or a train for somewhere: the Great White Father, Kent Cooper, has spoken at last.

Meanwhile, I'd better tell you a little something about "cablese"—cable messages. Just "GREENE ASSOCIATED LONDON" will reach me. And although it lacks the feeling of "WHAT HAS BECOME OF YOU" it will mean the same thing to me if you knock that into three words: "WHATS BECOME YOU."

You see, we eliminate all prepositions and almost all inactive verbs where the meaning is clear. I'll give you an example of how we cablese messages to Nyk:

"ADDISABAB EMPEROR DJIBOUTIWARDED MORNING LEAVING CAPITAL GRIP MARAUDERS WHO PILLAGED FIRED TOWN SPREAD DEATH DESTRUCTION STOP EXDAWN REIGN TERROR RAGED STREETS AMERICAN OTHER FOREIGN RESIDENTS FLED SAFETY LEGATIONS STOP EVENING TOWN FLAMES STOP STRAY BULLETS EXRIOTING LOOTERS SPATTERED AGAINS WALLS UNISTATES LEGATION WHENCE HUDDLED BODIES SLAIN VICTIMS COULD PLAINLY SEEN STOP MANY PRAYED TONIGHT PROARRIVAL ITALIAN TROOPS SAVE THEM EXTERRIBLE FATE HANDS UNRESTRAINED NATIVES STOP UNHOPE IMMEDIATE RELIEF SIGHT."

It would come out in the papers like this:

Addis Ababa (AP)—Emperor Haile Selassie left for Djibouti, the capital of the French colony in East Africa, this morning, leaving Ethiopia's capital in the grip of marauders who pillaged and set fire to the town and spread death and destruction.

From dawn, a reign of terror raged in the streets and American and other foreign residents fled to the safety of their legations. This evening, the town was in flames. Stray bullets from the rioting looters spattered against the walls of the United States Legation, and from there the huddled bodies of slain victims could be plainly seen.

Many prayed, tonight, for the arrival of the Italian troops to save them from a terrible fate at the hands of the unrestrained natives. No immediate hope of relief was in sight.

In cablese, those 69 cable words become 130 when they come out in the newspapers—not counting punctuation marks such as the "stops" which you have to put in to indicate the end of a sentence.

Here's a cablelogue:
PRO—for.
EX—from.
WARD—to, or went to.
UN—not.

That's about all you use, except that "more beautiful," for example, becomes "beautifuler" and "most lovely" becomes "loveliest"—"er" and "est" automatically signifying to the cable-desk editor in Nyk, who transcribes our copy, that we mean "more" or "most." Prepositions are eliminated unless they are necessary to make the context clear.

And so, BELOVEDEST MARYLOU DONT YOU CRY PROME PROEYEM COMIN EXSUNNYSOUTH WITH BANJO CROSS MY KNEE. And it's 4 A.M., and my coal-fire is glowing its last. In a lot of ways I sort of love you,

forever,

Roge

That Roge might be in New York within six months was incredible news. It was also unnerving. We would have to meet. The rapport we had felt during our Princeton weekend had been sustained and matured in our letters. I wondered if it would hold up face to face.

The children and I went back and forth to my parents' cottage at Virginia Beach beginning in May. It was a happy time for us, beach time with no schedules save that of high and low tide. Mary Lou and Tempie, in particular, were both in good health and sunshine. Roge, still an ocean's length away until the fall.

I was a little in love with him and with his life and in love with his version of me. We wrote each other that we were not the exciting version the other saw. He was not the dashing foreign correspondent leading a gay life. I was not the feminine ideal of patience and perseverance entertaining suitors from all over. But our versions of each other were strong and attractive and hard to unmask.

May 15, 1936

Mary Lou, dear:

What a grand, thrilling letter! Now I'm impatient, chafing,

terribly anxious to get back to New York. And your sweet promise—"I'll do my best to make up for your leaving London"—makes September seem an unbearably long time away.

I sail, according to latest marching orders, on September 15. The plan is that I'll stay in New York for about six months, letting the "big shot" executive editors look me over, and then shoot out into the foreign field once more. I hope so, at least; for I loathe New York as a place to live—or I did when I was there in 1930-31, working on the Herald-Tribune; it seemed the loneliest spot in all God's green acres. I was too poor, toiling at $40 a week, to have any fun, and I was never so happy as when I escaped back to California where you can, if you know how, live gloriously on almost nothing.

I'll be poor this time, too, until my raise comes through; but I know where I'm going now, and there seems to be some kind of a definite future, so it won't be so bad—not even counting the nearness to you, which, in happiness, could only be counted on an adding machine.

It is, believe me, Mary Lou, extraordinarily cheering to read that you're "not in the least likely to go off the deep end with a Southerner"—cheering, though slightly incredible, because you must have whole swarms of ardent young gentlemen eager to leap off high buildings or do mortal combat at your nodding, and it stands to reason that among them there must be some bold enough to simply sweep you up and carry you off over the horizon on a white charger. You sometimes say I idealize you too much—and as they say of the Englishman: "He puts woman on a pedestal, and uses it for a footstool!"—but all I know is that I'm that way about you: there is and has always been something about you that calls up splendid dreams and misty romantic vistas utterly unreal in this somewhat prosaic world. I am almost desperately afraid that the reality may be a little grim, because I want to call for you in a swift, sleek Isotta Frachini and shower you with exquisite orchids and sail away with you on a yacht, across moonlit waters to the South Seas—and the dreadful down-to-earth fact is that more likely it will be a meter-clicking cab, a gardenia and the Ship Cafe. It may be good earth, but I'm a pretty hopeless hankerer after star-dust . . .

In a sudden burst of ambition, I went into a huddle over the

105

typewriter early this morning and have been going hell-for-leather ever since—until I finished my work, about an hour ago, 9:30 P.M., and turned to this pleasanter field of writing you. I had a day off from the office, long since due for over-time work on King George's death; so I put on a new ribbon, cleaned the keys and let fly—revamped a 5,000-word short story which I posted to the magazine Esquire, and wrote two allegedly humorous pieces which are now in the mail en route to the magazine Judge.

The story has a grand plot and strong emotional drama, but helas! an unhappy ending and no love interest: consequently, it's no good for the popular maggies on the order of the SatEvePost, Collier's or Liberty; but Esquire goes in for semi-belles lettres stories of this type, so it may bring in a few hundred dollars.

Lord knows what inspired this sudden surge of energy— and I hope the Lord will keep it secret. At any rate, it's the first extra-curriculum work I've done in two or three years. I'm a lazy oaf, my dear. The cheek reddens with shame when I consider exactly how utterly damfool slothful I've been about my writing since I returned to the journalistic wars. Before that, when I was hungry and pretty desperately poor, out in Santa Monica in 1932, I worked like a dog and was beginning to make a little headway, collaborating with Agnes Christine Johnston on two stories which were published by Liberty—"The Unromantics" and "Home Papers, Please Copy"—and collaborating with her husband, Frank Dazey, on a movie story which came out under the title, "The Devil is Driving," starring Edmund Lowe. But once my cakes and ale were assured by my salary as a reporter on the San Francisco Call-Bulletin, I sluffed off the literary grind and began to enjoy living, if not life, thus leaving myself with a net score of approximately zero for the last three years. Maybe this is the dawn of a new era; I hope so.

I'm addressing this to your picturesquely down-South-romantic address on Pocahontas Drive, Virginia Beach, Virginia (Cavalier Shores)—how I love the bees-and-honeysuckle-and-cottonfields-yessuh roll of that combination of names! I only wish I could deliver the letter by hand, and see you come to the door:

I'm the new postman, ma'am.

Oh?

Yes, ma'am! And you sho' look pretty!

What's that?

I mean you got the loveliest eyes I ever—

Well, really—!

If it ain't an impertinence—

It is!

—I'd like to say you are simply, utterly and entirely glorious!

Go along now!

Here's a letter, from England.

Oh.

It hasn't got a stamp on it. I'll have to collect postage.

Well, how much?

I can't answer that, ma'am. I'll just have to leave it to your Southern hospitality.

You—you're not—?

Not?

Roge?

Yes.

Well, I'll be—(Noise of slamming door.)

CURTAIN

Tell me about this "swing music," Mary Lou. I saw it mentioned, very briefly, in one of the papers over here for the first time the other day—about how it is sweeping the United States like wild-fire. I suppose in another three months it will probably reach England. They're dreadfully slow about getting things here. They're just beginning to whistle about how the music goes 'round and around, on the streets, and it is now finally just about unanimous that if you push the middle valve down, the music comes out here.

What does "swing" mean—swinging from one tune or key into another, or what? We get pretty homesick for news from America: what's going on, what's the latest fad, the newest flip. It gets so bad sometimes, among the American foreign correspondents' colony here, that we get together over the nut-brown ale on Sunday nights and sing all the old numbers right down the line from "Down by the Old Mill Stream" to "On the

107

Sidewalks of New York"—with your correspondent rumbling away for dear life in a voice that alternately sounds like a lordly bullfrog and escaping steam. Along about 2 A.M., our repertoire begins to run out to such an extent that nobody quite knows the right words, but we soon learn some new ones from the surrounding tenants, who come to the door, all frowsy-eyed and mussy-haired and bath-robed, and announce categorically that our latest rendition about "the sons of the prophets are valiant and bold, and quite unaccustomed to fear" is making the night hideous. This pointed comment, opening up an entirely new line of thought, inevitably leads to a certain amount of debate, and I remember that at the last party, at Joe Driscoll's, the bath-robed intruder, with an horrific tremolo, wound up by making the night hideouser and hideouser as he tried, gallantly, I'll admit, to carry the bass-profundo of "Carry Me Back to Old Virginia" in an Oxford accent. As I recall it, somebody finally put a touch of alum in his highball, and after that he just looked like he was singing but he really wasn't at all.

My favorite, it goes without saying, is "Mary Lou" and I want to tell you I put real feeling into it when it comes to describing how all the bells in the steeple are waiting to ring—and it is no unusual thing to see my confreres break down and sob quietly at the utter despair and heartrending sadness in my voice. There is not a dry eye in the house, and to a man they come forward and say: "Roge, you must be brave!"

Well, Mary Lou dear, Big Ben just around the corner in Westminster is dolorously tolling midnight and I confess that after 15 solid hours perched over this keyboard I'm a little dizzy. Before Jimmy Walker was Mayor of New York, he wrote a song called "Will you love me in September as you did in May?"—and I wonder, too. Buenas noches, carissima mia.

Love, and love again,
Roge

May 25, 1936

Dearest Mary Lou:

Summer has struck this bleak, fog-ridden town at last—and

it is as breath-taking as a lovely girl in an Easter bonnet. The grey dreary days have suddenly given way to bright sparkling sunshine; the winter-time pall of black sooty smoke from a million chimneypots has vanished, and London, all at once, becomes enchanting. It is almost as though an ancient begrimed hag had been transformed into a maiden, all smiles and freshness and gaiety. In no other city that I have seen, including foggy San Francisco, is the change quite so startling.

I don't know why I go into rhapsodies about all this to you, except that it makes me feel so darn good—and because the bright summer days mean that now it will not be so long until fall, until September, and until I see you again. In fact, it will be just four months from today that I should land in New York, for I plan to leave here on September 15 and unless there is a great whooping rush for me to get back to New York I plan to return on one of the 10-day boats and simply relax on deck the whole voyage.

Things have been going almost too gloriously to be true for me this past week. To start it off, there came a letter from Wilson Hicks, the "big shot" feature editor of the whole AP service offering orchids for two stories I'd written—and believe me, those letters are just a little more rare than orchids. In the 18 months I've been with the AP, only one other man on the London staff has received a complimentary billet from Nyk; this made my sixth. Then Kendrick, one of the "Big Four" of Nyk editors and Kent Cooper's right-hand man, arrived in London—and it so happens that my good friend, Dave Sentner, star man of Hearst's International News Service in London, is a great friend of Kendrick, and Dave blew me to the skies to Kendrick. And to top it all, we were having a little after-golf party here in my flat Saturday night and one of the correspondents, Joe Driscoll, chief of the N.Y. Herald Tribune bureau in London, called up Kendrick about midnight and asked him to come on over. Kendrick said he was in pajamas, but over he came anyway—and he told Mother that from what he had seen and heard about me I'd "make a big hit in New York," which, of course, tickled me practically unconscious, because I have since heard that if Kendrick takes a liking to you you are practically made: that he has raised quite a few men up to the top in short order.

His drinking capacity, however, is better than mine. He called me up from his hotel the next evening and asked me to join a party having drinks in his room, but I just couldn't take it. It was only about 7:30, but I was already in bed. You see, we'd sat up until 4 A.M. and then I had to go to work at 9 A.M. Sunday, and there were many moments all day Sunday when I was afraid that I wouldn't live and then afraid that I would. This English ale is delightful, but it packs a boomerang that makes your head, the morning after, feel like 10,000 chipmunks quarreling over a nut. I'm afraid that I soaked up a good deal of it, too, for we came back from golf about five o'clock and drank for the next eleven hours, which might not be bad if I were in drinking trim, but I'd been high on the wagon for more than a week getting out a lot of free-lance work—including a short story, some stuff to Judge, and a polo article for The Spur.

This foreign correspondents colony is a hard-drinking bunch, although not much harder, I suppose, than any gathering of a Fourth Estate tribe; newspapermen, proverbially and perennially, seem to go in for bottled cheer in large quantities, and when you come to New York and we go on newspaper parties I guess you will see a certain amount of plain and fancy drinking. I don't know yet what your views are on this. I know that you are pretty religious and golly! for all I know you may be an ardent tee-totaller. I have forgotten, now, whether we drank at the Princeton prom, although I think we did, for it was just about that time, with the crew season ended and training over, that I had my first drink. I was 20 then, in 1924, and had only tasted liquor once before in my life—that was the previous summer when I was a counselor at a poor boy's camp on Long Island (they used to draft a lot of Andover men to act as counselors) and a bunch of us went down to Jamesport, L.I., nearby, and somebody bought a bottle of rye, and after three swigs from the bottle everything went all woozy and then blank and I decided I would never drink again if I survived this once, honest God and truly. But helas! the frailty of human will, for after Princeton, out in California, I did a fair amount of earnest drinking with the notable exception of nearly a year strictly on the wagon. I just wanted to see whether I could have as much fun at parties, stark sober, as when imbibing like everybody else: I found that you could, but that it gets infinitely tedious explaining what many people called the psychopathic twist of my mind in trying to be "different"—they stared at me as though I were a Man from Mars, an anti-social being, or else definitely barmy.

All this leads up to the thing that amazes me: how very little we know of each other. All we have, really, is our letters and 48 hours visibly together a long time ago. Judging by your letters and my memories of that little time, you are something very extra splendid and to be cherished. Certainly we "clicked," or it seemed to me, in those rapid kaleidoscopic moments of 12 years ago. Perhaps we shall again, but it will surely be one of the most extraordinary meetings since time began: I mean, we will be almost complete strangers, on the surface, with a mighty intimacy struggling underneath. The idea just about turns my heart over in a shaky throb—the mad romance of it all, like a skyrocket flinging sparks against the sky at night . . . and like a skyrocket, too, perhaps thudding to earth with the sparkless disillusion of reality. For I am pretty deathly afraid that whatever ideas of glamor you may have conjured up about me will suffer a shock when you see me as just a pretty average guy with a white patch over one eye and a moustache that never has nor ever will make anyone mistake me for Ronald Coleman. Good Lord! maybe I'd better just stay abroad and write you without ever seeing you. Beethoven, you know, did that—wrote love letters for years and years to a lovely woman who worshipped his music, but never saw her . . .

Well, September is a long way off. I know I shall remain faithful because I have never loved anyone so sincerely or for so long, but then I have been through a lot of bachelor summers while you—well, Mary Lou, I cannot rate my chances very high, somehow, of your surviving very long under a moon on Cavalier Shores . . . unless the waves, tumbling in with their old sad song, should remind you of a guy named Greene way off beyond the rim of the sky.

I started to write something, on the previous sheet, when the doorbell rang and some friends roared in—and that was the end of letter-writing for the night.

Today, Tuesday, has gone by like a streak. Spent most of the morning writing a long cable on the Arab-Jew riots in

Palestine. Then a big luncheon of American foreign correspondents association at the Savoy, where we had Major Clement R. Attlee, leader of His Majesty's Opposition in the House of Commons, for speaker. Quite a doggy affair, with footman in scarlet coat and knee breeches to announce us as we enter the cocktail salon.

This afternoon, I toiled on a variety of stories, ranging from a shipwreck in the North Sea in which six men were drowned, to a feature on a 20-year-old girl who "died" in the dental chair— her heart actually stopped beating for seven minutes—but they resuscitated her and went right on extracting teeth before she woke up—24 teeth in all.

Must wind this up now to get it on the boat-train for the S.S. *Queen Mary* on her maiden voyage. I only wish I were aboard— with the first stop Cavalier Shores!

Lots of love, Mary Lou,
Ever,
Roge

I saw Scott Fitzgerald at a party. It was unexpected, but not unlikely since he often visited his cousin Cecilia at the beach. He had placed Zelda in a private hospital near Asheville that spring and was spending much of his summer up there when not in Baltimore.

Scott was in bad shape. Alcoholism had destroyed his health. The financial and emotional strain of his relationship to Zelda coupled with his devotion to his daughter, Scottie, had worn him down. He appeared to have given up, which was so unlike the Scott I had first met in December of 1926. The belief in the happy ending was gone.

The meeting saddened me greatly, though he was happy and surprised to see me. He wanted me to sit by him, and he held my hand. He had tears in his eyes and did not want me to leave. Perhaps I was a reminder to him of that moment in his life when he was riding high—when his books were read, when he and Zelda were still together, though not without trouble, when life still held possibilities.

In the decade since our first meeting, he had lost that hope, and it was very hard to look at him and know that. He was a dear man. Much later, I read something he had written that has stayed with me: "I left my capacity for hoping on the little roads that lead to Zelda's sanitarium."

I wrote to Roge about seeing Scott. I thought how strange it was that I had spent more time face to face with Scott Fitzgerald than I had with Roge.

June 15, 1936

My dearest Mary Lou:

I am selfish. I long to hear from you every day. Impossible, of course: the boats do not run that often—and I could hardly expect you to keep a diary just for my distant benefit. I am afraid I have all the tingling curiosity about you that our New York editors, the "pulse of the great American public," have about King Edward VIII.

For example, they have just sent a request asking for a series of yarns dealing with a thousand and one details of his personality. They want to pierce "the divinity which doth hedge a king"; they want to know what size hat he wears, the color of his hair, what color ties he prefers, how much and what he drinks, is his temper still as flaming as when he was Prince of Wales, what is a typical day in his life from rising-hour to bed-time? Will he marry? Whom? And a thousand and one other little intimate details.

I think I shall write them back asking for a series of yarns, built on the same order, about M.L.A. Or maybe it would be best to wait until I get back, and interview you myself.

"Mrs. Ryland?"
"Yes."
"How do you do? I am Roger Greene—from The Associated Press."
"Well?"
"Sit down, Mrs. Ryland. I want to have a heart-to-heart talk with you."

113

"How you talk."

"How am I doing?"

"You're under-done. In fact, half-baked. I would say about another ten minutes in the oven—"

"I don't need an oven, honey. You burn me up and down."

"Carry on."

"This is serious. Mrs. Ryland, what do you think of love?"

"Are you mad?"

"No, just hysterical. Listen—"

Oh, it's no use. I have to have the subject in front of me before I can interview them. Well, that won't be so terribly long now, measured in hard and fast units of days and weeks: I sail just three months from today. And then—New York! Mary Lou! A whirling new life!!

Your description of the "dark cloud" journey from Bluefield to Virginia Beach was rollicking gorgeous. A grand line that— about the "children with a bad case of the wiggles."

But hell, honey, I thought you were poor. And here, out of a clear sky, you tell me about taking along three Negroes and a cook and nurse and your mother's chauffeur to drive you down to what you had previously described to me as a little beach cottage but which turns out to have five bedrooms and three baths not counting the servants' quarters.

I guess I should have guessed that your riding, golf, parties and traipsing around and about all over the South—the new car and all—couldn't be done on free-air at the nearest service station. Still, you had told me you were pretty hugely hard up—going to become a secretary or something.

Now everything is changed. I'm a poor damn reporter, and suddenly my dreams lie in ashes . . .

Still, I want to see you. There is no one in the world I have ever wanted to see more.

I am feverish to be back. I love London. As Dr. Johnson said: "Sir, when a man is tired of London he is tired of life." But I am restless, burning up, to drive into the next new chapter of the Greene saga. You mention my "nomad life." It seems to be true. About August, 1937, I expect to be in Moscow. Charlie Nutter, one of the fellows on the London staff, just about my best friend here, has just been ordered to Moscow for a year, and having heard me say that I'd like to go to Russia for the AP, he said that when he leaves there, he'll pull strings with his friend Kent Cooper to have me follow him on the Muscovite trail. Charlie was Chief of Bureau in Mexico City, and now becomes Chief of Bureau in Moscow—and is headed for big things. He seems to think that I am, too; but the darn thing is that I'm still pretty young and worse than that, I've only been on the AP for 17 months while he's been a staff correspondent, roving all over the world, for about nine years. He's now 35, and he thinks enough of my writing judgment to come and ask me to edit his copy, which is the highest compliment you can pay in this cut-throat game where every writer could cheerfully kill anybody who cuts his copy or even questions an adjective.

England is beautiful now. Showers of sun, and showers of rain. Never really hot, but green, and clear skies where for month after month there has been only bleak zinc overhead or fog. I went out to the country yesterday, down Surrey way, to a house-party, mostly English, where we played furious tennis hour after hour on a lovely grass court surrounded by fragrant gardens—still going strong at 7:30, with the English sun blazing strong to the last. I found my alleged "cannon-ball" serve still smoking beautifully, although it was only the second time I had played since California days, but my ground strokes were depressing.

We halted for tea at five—the young son of the household, a red-rosy cheeked lad of five, trumpeting "Tea-time! Tea-time!!" with all the clarion vitality of Gabriel blowing his horn for the Last Judgment. They go at their tea very seriously over here. And what a tea! The table was groaning under great platters of dainty sandwiches, scones, crumpets, strawberry jam, whipped cream, cakes galore, pastry, cold meats—and, yes, and tea, which gives the name to this gargantuan repast but which is only an odd item.

Lord, how they do stow it away, too. I couldn't. I was too intent on tennis, and played three more sets which I fell none the better for today; indeed, my ancient bones are creaking right heartily and I feel pretty limp all over, though I should be in fair shape for I've played a lot of golf.

After tennis came cocktails, then a light supper, and then we played charades—not, I understand, "char-aydes" but "sharahds," they call it over here. Anyway, it was my first experience of the game, and I thought, "Oh, Lord, how utterly silly! Only children play that." And Charlie Nutter and I churlishly refused to be drawn for sides: we said, "We're reporters. We'll write it up for the London 'Times.' You charade all you want." So the first side went out, and when they completed their act, the guessing team (about a dozen) sat around with chins in hand. The host had explained to me how the game works, and something apparently clicked in my grey-matter because in thirty seconds, seeing everybody look blank, I said, "I've got it! It's NOSEGAY!" And it was. They made a horrible fuss over me; I blushed furiously and wished I'd kept my mouth shut. You know, pleased as punch at being bright, and all that, but feeling pretty much like a glump. I don't know how to explain, exactly, what a glump is, but it is half-way between a chump and a poodle dog.

Our host was a "City Man" —the English equivalent of New York's Wall Street—and has millions, but he is the soul of charm and it was glorious fun. Mother and I are asked again for next Sunday and Mother has made such a hit with the hostess, Mrs. Barnard, that they want her to come out and stay. She may do it. Then we could close our apartment, I could bunk with Frank Kelley, of the New York Herald Tribune, who has chambers in the Inner Temple, and so save money to help pay my fare home. I've got to save it somehow starting soon, though I've sold two polo articles to "The Spur" magazine for which I'm getting $125—for about three hours' work, which isn't bad.

Esquire rejected my story, with the brief notation, "Not our type." Too dismal, I'm afraid. Surprised to hear that Charlie Robbins is still writing—you said he hit Esquire. Last time I saw him was in New York, in 1930, when he was pounding out horror-stuff for the Hearst Sunday maggy section. He was my brother Bill's best friend at both Andover and Princeton; belonged to the same fraternity at Andover, Alpha Gamma Xi, which harbored all the three brothers Greene.

Tell me more about Scott Fitzgerald. His private life sound inutterably sad—wreckage . . . Judging by his early novels, he has more sense of beauty in words than any man, of all time, I have ever read—and that covers a good deal of reading. It seems a pity that he has turned to SatEvePost pot boilers instead of writing novels with a little more of the wistful, yearning beauty of his youth than the coldly glittering sophistication of his maturity. I have read most of his SatEvePost stories and hated him for writing them, although God knows he probably sweated and struggled enough to write them without my heaping anathemas on his head. Lately, however, his short stories seems to have regained, marvelously regained, that gossamer touch of magic and poignant beauty which marked his earlier writing so indelibly.

If you see him again, please tell him that perhaps the other side of "This Side of Paradise" is not his forte.

And so to bed, Mary Lou—3,000 miles this side of Paradise. Please rush pictures of yourself and the babes.

Ever,

Roge

It was strangely upsetting to me that Roge thought I was unattainable because I was a rich Southern girl of a certain class and he was just a struggling reporter born of the Midwest. The plot was "Gatsby-esque," which was fine fiction, but we were real and not Fitzgerald characters.

Scott's real life tragedy had affected me. I did not want Roge's dreams to lie in ashes. I let him know I was certainly not rich, though I did not say how far I was from poor. We needed to write facts now, not fiction. I wanted him to come back.

Monday,

June 22, 1936

Mary Lou, my very dearest:

All day long, your letter has been singing in my heart . . .

It came, as gladness and fresh beauty should come, in the morning; and then, through the fine brisk day at Wimbledon, covering the international tennis tournament, I stole quick glances at it again, between sets, in a most ridiculously sentimental

Victorian fashion. You say sweet things, my dear—inutterably sweet; and when you write that you have "been caught red-handed day-dreaming," I wonder if you haven't been seized too with this same weird madness that now seems to have me practically crackers about you. Or so it is reported, according to latest dispatches from the front.

I don't know whether to believe dispatches from the front or not. Things are pretty topsy-turvy there right now. I mean to say, I do not know whether I am coming or going: there seems to be a certain amount of shell-shock, acute palpitation of the heart and an atrocious tendency to sing something about wanting to be carried back to West Virginia.

FLASH BULLETIN EOS—"I'M A-COMING SOUTH!"

EOS stand for Extraordinary Service, and when the AP or INS or UP flashes that symbol out over their networks or wires, it means a big story coming—and I wonder how it will read, after September.

You say, "The waves tumbling in with their old song have reminded me of you as you asked"—and, Mary Lou, honestly, I am going down to the shore and speed the tempo of those waves, lash them into mountains until you will hear them even after you have left those enchanting Cavalier Shores. Oh, Lord, if I could only have been there with you! The sample daily program sounds like heaven—a lazy day, and then, as you write, "dancing at the Beach Club—on the deck, in the moonlight, under the stars . . ." Hey, listen, Mary Lou! are you deliberately trying to drive me barmy, a dish for 10,000 squirrels?

"You see," sez you, "What I am trying to do is break down all the resistance you have about coming back." So, okay. If I ever had any resistance, it is now worn to a flutter. If they try to counter-order me anywhere else than New York in September—as there is now some talk of doing—I'll just have to chalk one up to destiny and walk out on everything in this career racket. I've done it before, though not over a girl; but then—and this is the maddest part of all—I have never felt the dizzy reeling glory before about a girl such as exists between you and me, or at least me. I want to be everything for you: I want to be famous and rich and more than anything I want to be the kind of man you'd like to have around you pretty often or even more often than that.

I want, if possible, to contribute to your happiness, because I am never more cheered than when I receive a letter from you that tells me you are having a fine gay time. You were pretty bleak there, for a while last winter; and now the change in your letters, the gradual drift from subdued chrysalis to free-winging life once more, is pretty darn splendid, my dear. You've no idea, I think, what a bright new tempo you have struck and what a changed person you have become during the past few months. The whole tone of your letters is different. It is a contrast of the deep river and the mountain brook that has bells in its voice. Six months ago, I believe, you were a little weary of life. I don't know. This is all conjecture. It is impossible to know much about you, really, until I hear your voice. But I think, reading between the lines, that you felt an odd desperation back there when we first began to write again. Now there is no desperation. Now there is a wild sweet song of life singing in you, and everything is pretty dandy on earth.

Still, this writing back and forth of ours is a rather desperate thing. I cannot feel happy over it, because I can never quite feel entitled to say the things I want to say. Always there is a feeling of absolute fantasy, as though it were a chapter from a Michael Arlen novel. I worried like the very devil over the salutation to this letter. I wanted to bring you nearer with a little stronger opening phrase, written on a typewriter here in my flat, in London, 3,000 miles away, and yet it practically sawed my soul apart to write "Mary Lou, my very dearest" because—oh, not because you're not a whole brimming-over lot dearer than that, but because decorum seems to demand a lot of restraint. Do you see what I mean? I think, each time I write you: "Well, I'd better just hide what I feel and be pretty stiff so that she won't feel qualms about the whole thing, because the whole thing is crazy!" And it is crazy, except that I know a parallel case of phantasmagore: Rob Bundy, of the famous tennis-playing Bundy family (May Sutton Bundy, Wimbledon champion 1904-6, and Tom Bundy, United States doubles champion with Maury McLoughlin for two years) came abroad about six years ago. He had gone to school in Santa Monica Calif., with a beautiful little kid named Marge Flowers, but there wasn't much in it. Then, while Rob was in England, they started writing, casually, sporadically, with increasing

119

frequency, until finally Marge came over and all at once the bells of St. Dunstan's-in-the-Strand began to ring—and the last I saw of them, in Santa Monica, they were the most sparkling couple in Southern California, and always ragging the hell out of me because I was still a bachelor. It seems to be a habit with married couples . . .

Yes, I know "I'm Putting All My Eggs in One Basket." Gayle Talbot, our European sports editor and the biggest rake in Europe—a funny little guy from Texas, with never less than 17 women on his trail, in Germany, in France, in Cairo, in these British Isles—is forever singing it across the desk from me at the office. It is pretty awful. I mean, his voice; he couldn't carry a tune in a bucket. But I know the song. And I know, now, what it might mean . . .

It must have been glorious fun down there at Virginia Beach, Mary Lou, with your guests arriving Thursday and trooping off Monday—some weekend! I'd like to meet your Iron Duke, because you like him so much and because he must be quite a lad to have sponsored a couple of good-looking guys like you and Frank. I only met Frank two or three times, but even before I met you I put him up as one of my top major gods of the campus. He was a junior, then, I believe, and it was just about the biggest thrill of my days as a frosh when Waltuh Hale introduced us, and Frank a little while later called me "Roge." That's a long time ago, but I have never forgotten it in the apparently bigger world outside of college. For example, last night I went to a party at the Grosvenor House with Dick Arlen, Jobyna Ralston, Eugene Pallette and a small handful of allegedly famous foreign correspondents sitting at the table, and all the celebrities came up and spoke to us, including the magnificent if slightly flamboyant Lord Castlerosse in his Beau Brummel outfit; but on the whole, I treasure, a lot more, the kindness of Frank condescending to say hello to me, on the campus, that I do the so-called glamor of parking with newspaper headline figures.

London is sweltering now. California's hottest days simply aren't in it with the heat over here, once it gets started—a muggy, wet heat that just about stifles you. Luckily, I'll be lolling out at Wimbledon, instead of baking in our Fleet-street office, for the next ten days—and after Wimbledon come the Davis Cup

120

matches, so I shaln't be seeing much of the office for the next month. I don't know if you have seen Wimbledon or not, on your junkets abroad, but it is a fine garden spot—flowers, beautiful lawns and cool deep shade in the Centre Court grandstand, which is where I work, if you could call it work. That's one of the charms of this newspaper racket: you get the best seats and occasionally write a few odd paragraphs and have messenger boys whizzing around at your beck and call, and you get paid for it! And while other people gape at the stars and feel immensely fluttered to get an autograph, you chat with them for an interview—and how they love it! Most tennis stars, or stars in any sport, are pretty much publicity-hounds. Helen Jacobs, for example, calls me up whenever she has news about herself.

Another week-end down in Kent, playing tennis, eating enormous English teas, more tennis, a swim in a garden pool, cold supper with ale, good talk, then back to London late. There is something very pleasant about the English country gentlemen life. It may not be really living, but it is grand fun in a quiet way and I would like to devote a lot of time to it. My tennis is pretty sour: it has been about six years since I played at all earnestly, back in Santa Monica: about the only relic left of my game is a hard-socking service, which fairly shredded the net and left it gaping large holes at the end of the day.

Haven't played golf in weeks. Tennis is much better for me, anyway, because golf doesn't seem to do a thing towards stream-lining my waistline—and it rather needs it! I'm up to about 190, which is a good deal even for my height of 6'1". I played five roaring sets, under a grilling sun, and am sure I lost a good five pounds; but darn it, I'm afraid I put it all back on again with the quantities of strawberries and rich Devonshire cream and sandwiches and cakes and scones at the tea interval. It is a miracle English people are so thin: you would think, judging the way they go at their tea and all that goes with it, that they'd be practically roly-poly. Instead, they have waistlines like grasshoppers.

I'm an ardent Rooseveltian too, Mary Lou, even though I was born and raised a Republican. But I've voted Democrat in my two elections so far, and I shall certainly vote for FDR this fall. In my notion, he is the greatest thing that ever happened to

America, standing head and shoulders above Washington, Lincoln and—with a bow to Bluefield—General Robert E. Lee, suh!

Now 3 A.M., and as the barmaids announce at the closing hour: "Time, gentlemen—please!" My dearest love to you, darling . . .

Roge

June 30, 1936

Mary Lou dearest:

Mid-summer madness or something, I think, must have seized me; for my last letter to you still hasn't left England—it goes on the S.S. *Queen Mary* tonight, I believe—and here I am writing you again.

Still, that seems to be how I feel about you . . .

BULLETIN: The patient is making a gallant fight, hospital attaches said, but some alarm is felt over the increasing fever.

ADD BULLETIN: Physician shook their heads. "The case," they said, "is completely baffling. The patient lacks appetite, is flushed, haggard, but shows no traceable symptoms. He seems to be slowly going barmy. Yes, it is very, very sad."

Oh, Lord, visitors . . .

Back again. An English girl. Blonde, blue-eyed, long cigarette-holder; pretty dreadfully English, all Oxford drawl and "my deah-h-h"—you know how they drag out the "ah-h-h" until they're darn near gargling? Two hours wasted.

English girls! Well, they have lovely peach-bloom complexions, with almost no rouge, but their hair looks ratty, all scraggly, and the conscious striving of their attempts at sex appeal are pretty blatant. They are so jealous of American women, and all trying to ape Hollywood movie stars. They have read columns and columns about Garbo and Crawford and Harlow, and how furiously, how desperately, how inanely coyly they are trying to copy them! Boldish vixens, they are, too. Merely as a curiosity, not because I want to impress you—(Lord knows, I shall have a difficult enough time trying to do that next fall!)—and anyway this is Leap Year: but I've had two bombshell proposals from English gals this year. Right smack out of the blue. Really, they're funny—except that is a pretty bleak thing, in England, the devil

of a time girls have in finding a suitable man; and when they
do . . .

Well, when they do, it is pretty drastically a case of: "Run
for your lives, men!"

As they say in cricket, they go "all out"—which is about the
English equivalent of Babe Ruth knocking six home runs in a
single game. The epitome of effort.

An American man over here becomes practically a demi-
god. Englishmen are so cold, so hostilely cold, darn near brackish,
to their women that the poor creatures simply swoon at a touch
of gentleness. Then, too, they have all heard that American men
are so good, so friendly to their women, that they stampede
anything with a male American accent. Perhaps that is part of
London's charm, although not for me: after two years here, I feel
like breaking out the Stars and Stripes and shouting from the
rooftops every time I meet an American gal. There is simply no
comparison. I can't quite define it, but our American girls have it
a thousand times over anything I've seen over here so far. I may
be breaking all the traditional rules of masculinity in letting you
know this, but I secretly enjoy letting an American girl twist me
around her fingers (as they always do, Lord help us!) but if an
English girl tries the same delightful (in America) tactics, I only
think: "Oh, dear, how dreadfully amateurish! Ho-hum." I
suppose it is still the aftermath of the war years, still the shortage
of eligible men, still the too deadly intentness of the English female
of the species. There is nothing I more deeply and keenly
appreciate than frankness; but it isn't frankness here: it is as
driving-to-the-goal a proposition as Caesar crossing the Rubicon
or Hannibal the Alps—and heaven help the elephants and Richard
Halliburton!

This week has been grand, darling—out at Wimbledon
covering the tennis tournament, a grand soft job; tomorrow I go
up to Henley, to cover the big regatta; then Thursday to
Newmarket for the horse races, then back on Friday and Saturday
to Henley again. Immediately afterwards, my vacation starts—
two weeks. I was planning to go abroad. Planning, most recently,
on a motorbike junket through the Black Forest of Germany: I
wanted, too, to go to Brittany, and down to the south coast of
Spain. I wanted to hit Paris for 24 hours, and dash to Berlin for

an evening in the biergartens with some of my friends there. Instead, I shall remain in London and play golf and tennis; because I've got to save up my boat fare home in September and get some new clothes with which to make a shining debut, if possible, to the Nyk office. I'm getting almighty ragged, and smart clothes mean a lot in this racket, and the next six months will mean make-or-break for me. So, I'll have to forget my dreams for a while, and I guess I can stand it: I'm thirty-two, and there are a lot of glorious years ahead when there'll be money to do things. Everything in me burns, though, now: it looks so far away. Patience! patience!

And so to bed, with Big Ben chiming midnight. My love to you, Mary Lou . . .

Roge

July 4, 1936

Dearest Mary Lou:

Just back from the farewell boat party to Charley Nutter, sailing at midnight to become our new Chief of Bureau in Moscow—a grand promotion for him, leading up to his becoming Bureau Chief in Paris perhaps a year from now and a big-time future ahead.

He took me aside and told me that he knows—his emphasis—I can succeed him a year hence if I want to. Did my heart stand still! He's several years older than I am, about 35, I should say, has been in the AP nearly ten years to my two, and is very brilliant indeed . . . and I am hugely happy about it. About everything. And how seemingly perfect everything is working out.

Almost the only thing I remember from my courses in physics, both at Andover and Princeton, is the law that "To every action there is an equal and opposite reaction"—and I've found that holds pretty generally true of everything in life. So on that basis, I've probably got a lot of bleak disappointments ahead somewhere to provide the reaction.

But now! It's really a little too good, too smooth! Glowing words about my work here. Back to New York in September and a new thrust at an adventurous new world. Most of all, the climax of this Haroun-al-Raschid story-book romance of tu et moi.

What strange, unfathomable prospects ahead!

But first, your grand letter! I stopped off on my way from the Henley regatta to the Russian boat, despairing of there being any letter; for although I haven't been into the office at all this week—what with the Henley regatta and the American Kentucky Derby winner, Omaha, running at Newmarket in the Princess of Wales stakes Thursday—I'd phoned in every night to see if there was any mail. And there it was—a nice thick envelope. With the cab and a crowd waiting, I didn't have time to read it then, but as soon as we got aboard the ship I slipped off to a corner of the lounge and read it ravenously, and all the newspaper clippings, and particularly lingered on the gay sunny-smiling picture of you and the adorable little Tempie and Mary Lou II "in the courtyard of their cottage on Cavalier Shores" —darn near poetry! They are beautiful children, Mary Lou, and it would be fatuous to comment on where they get their beauty from. An enchanting picture: what a thrill if it could only come to life!

Witt Hancock, I understand, arrives in London in a few days now. Extraordinary—his coming from Bluefield, of all places in the world! I'll certainly welcome him and try to make him feel at home. Another chap named Wingate, also from the NYK office, is coming over with him—both replacements for the old staff which is rapidly breaking up. Charlie Nutter to Russia. Al Wilson, who went from the London bureau to cover the Addis Ababa business, has now gone back to NYK. Another staff member, Oscar Leiding, is going back soon. And I'm sailing September 15. Only two of the old staff will be left then, so Hancock and Wingate will have splendid chances to show what they can do.

Wish you had sent the other picture of yourself—the one you withdrew at the last minute; but anyway, please do send another. The "shock," as you call it, is terrifically pleasant. Believe me, darling, you carry a high voltage!!

The beach cottage certainly looks most delightful. It reminds me so much of the movie colony cottages on the beach front at Santa Monica, where Doug Fairbanks, Mary Pickford, Irving Thalberg and Norma Shearer, Marion Davies, and others live in a row along with half a dozen of the smarter beach clubs. I had about five glorious years of it ... great days marching drowsily ...

getting bronzed and hard in the hot sun, playing volleyball, swimming, lazing, regretfully watching the sun dip in a final rainbow plunge beyond the blue, then dancing—and up with another radiant day. Life hit its zenith of enjoyment for me then, and in a way it seems a pity that the ole debbil ambition sent me roaming afield in search of a Golden Fleece which was already at hand. Still, if I hadn't come abroad, I'd probably never have heard from you again, and life would have been vastly different. It is curious and exciting what you can make of life, or let it make of you. It seems to be a pretty clear-cut case of guide or be guided. It is a little hard for me, looking back, to believe in destiny. I've torn the fabric of my life so often, cast one pattern aside to find a newer and bigger design for living. All I have to show for it, so far, is a burning restlessness, an impatience to "get on with it," whereas if I had stayed in Santa Monica, instead of barging off to New York in 1929, I would probably have been contentedly settled as a solid citizen with a house, wife, children, car, golf and beach clubs and a serious sense of self-importance. None of these treasures are mine—nothing solid: and the only compensation, a fairly adventurous career. Sometimes I look back ruefully at what might have been; at other times, I tingle with the prospects for the future— the uncertainty, the suspense, the promise fulfilled and unfulfilled, the carnival of living. Maybe you know the answer to it all . . .

More again. Thanks so much for the pictures, Mary Lou. I enclose the snapshot of the two great little kids and their granddad, who looks like a perfect peach. I love Tempie's smile: what a honey she is!

That goes double for you, from me,

Roge

That July, Tempie's asthma became worse with more frequent and longer episodes. We nursed her at our beach cottage with plenty of rest and home remedy, but one night her struggle for air was too much and I took her to the hospital nearby in Norfolk.

She had never been hospitalized for her asthma. They put her under an oxygen tent, all the while speaking in a hush. I wanted to know the prognosis. They told me her condition was serious.

I stayed with her day and night. She will be four years old in another month, I told myself as I looked at her frail figure on the bed.

"Tempie, you are going to be fine," I told her over and over, and she would find the strength to nod and smile. Each breath was a gasp, and I was hypnotized by the rise and fall of her chest. I had never been so scared.

"Tempie, we will have a fine birthday next month."

"Tempie, Mama is right here."

"Tempie."

July 17, 1936

Dear Mary Lou:

That sounds a little brusque.

Just "Dear Mary Lou"—

But I want it, I think, to sound brusque. Because if I said "My dear" or "Dearest Beloved" or even (with a very soft voice) "Darling Mary Lou"—no matter how I said it, it still would not tell you about the funny aching happy reverence in my heart about you.

So it is better, I guess, to be short. Gruff. You see, for the first time in my life, you have brought me something a little too big for words. That is what your last letter has done to me, Mary Lou: it is so immeasurably human: it is such a glorious cry from the wilderness of deep emotion. "I can't tell you how I feel," you said. "All I know to-night is that I want my baby child to get well soon—and for you to come back—"

All I know to-night is . . .

Two things. Tempie, and me. And, oh, Mary Lou, I am touched, way down deep, that you could seem to love me enough even to spare a thought about me in the same breath with darling Tempie. I suppose I shouldn't say this: but it is true that from the photographs I've adored Tempie just a little more than Mary Lou II., maybe because Tempie looks so much like you as I remember you, with the same gay teasing smile and the happy gift of laughter . . .

At first, all suddenly, I was frightened. I mean, when I saw the letter-head on your envelope: "Norfolk General Hospital."

I'm still on holiday, until next Wednesday. But I barged into the office last night, dog-tired from 36 holes, after calling up and learning that there was over-seas mail in my box. "Where from?" I asked. Bud Johns was on the City Desk. "Jus' minute," he said. And called, "Oh, boy! Look in Mr. Greene's box and see where his letters are from . . . New York, San Francisco, Santa Monica, and—wuzzat? Norf'k? Norfolk, Virginia!" "Huh?" I said, "Norfolk, Virginia? I don't know anybody . . ." "Yah?" he said, "that must be that gal from Bluefield!" "Oh!" I said, and ran lickety-split to the 'tube, at Hammersmith, near the golf course, to get there quick as could be.

It took a long time to get there. It seemed like a lot of hours. I had waited pretty long to hear from you, though no blame, honey, for I can't say how much I thank you for writing me at all amid such distress. Anyway, I shot upstairs, dove into my mailbox and sorted the envelopes in a rush. I saw your handwriting. And I saw that heading "Norfolk General Hospital" and I thought, "Oh, God, something has happened to her! An automobile accident . . . an airplane crash . . . she fell while riding . . . Oh, God, oh my God!" I snagged a fingernail into the flap and ripped it open, and just then Bud, alone on the City Desk, at night, with the staff gone, hollered: "Oh, Roge! I know you're on vacash, but I'm in a jam with all this copy coming in—up to my neck— would you give me a hand!" The trans-continental trunk lines were shrilling: Berlin and Moscow both calling in at once, and I could see a whole pile of ticker copy heaped on the desk, with poor Bud trying to crack out a late night story about the attempted assassination of King Edward. So I swore, thrust your letter burning into my breast pocket, and set to work—two hot and heavy hours of it without a second's pause, except that half the time my mind was slithering away from new reports about the assassination attempt and the running story from the House of Commons and the Reuter's copy from Geneva about the new Locarno Powers conference and some Yugo-Slavian air minister who was successfully assassinated and a myriad other news reports from all over the globe, everyone of which had to be read and judged whether it was worth cabling on to New York—and all the time, my brain whirling with the dread sinking uncertainty of what that address of "Norfolk General Hospital" meant to the

128

one girl on earth who mattered, or ever had mattered, or ever shall matter. At last, a few minutes before midnight, the tickers quieted down, the trans-continental trunk lines stopped screaming with calls from our various bureaus, Bud wiped sweat from his brow, slammed the last "take" of his story into the copy hook, yowled "Copy boy-ee-e-e-ee!" like a banshee, and said, "Well, thank God, you came in!" "Sure!" I said, and managed a grin. "It's been a big night," Bud said, "I'd have been swamped, honest to God. What made you come down, and you on vacation?" "Oh," I said, "I just thought I'd look in." And I wanted to scream at him, "You goddam fool, haven't you ever been in love? That's why I came in. I came in to see if there might be a letter from my girl. That's why!" But you don't say those things, out loud.

Then I left. In the hall, downstairs, I opened your letter at last, and I guess maybe I'm not a hard-boiled newspaperman after all, because all at once, as the lines of your letter flowed into my brain and all down through me, I almost wanted to cry, Mary Lou, about Tempie and about you and about the swell things you said. ". . . and for you to come back," you said, and "—that your return is the thing I am looking forward to more than you can possibly realize . . ." And I don't know, and maybe it doesn't matter so much, whether you really meant all that but just felt it, in the storm of your weary emotions, just then. But I am glad you said it, Mary Lou; I am happy because you felt it, even for a moment.

It's going to be a funny fall.

Roge

July 20, 1936

Darling Mary Lou:

Less than two months now—before sailing!

And Lord, I'm hugely excited already about seeing you, talking to you, going around and about with you! How far is Bluefield from New York? How long does it take by train? How much does it cost? How in the deuce am I going to see much of you when I have to work and you living so far away? Couldn't you possibly move to New York? Get a job there? Visit somebody?

129

Patience, boy, patience!

U.S. mail today, but no letter from you. I'm back at the office. Cut my vacation two days short because of all the flurry over hell cracking wide open over in Spain. Lots of news streaming in from border towns around Spain—Lisbon, Gibraltar, French towns—but the wires, both cable and telephone, are silent to Madrid. Late this afternoon it was reported that the rebels had captured Madrid. Nobody knows what is happening, except that it is a real revolution. The funny thing is that one of our London staff correspondents, "Pete" Peterson, just left Saturday night for San Sebastien, Spain. "I'm going down there on the beach sands and just rest, in peace and absolute quiet, for ten solid days," he said. Poor Pete! San Sebastien, according to dispatches this afternoon, is one of the hot-spots of the fighting—and I'm afraid that if Pete gets any of his rest on the beach it will only be found by setting up lodgings as a clam, well under the sand, below the whine of bullets.

It will probably be days before I hear from you, I guess. I wanted to cable you, as soon as I read your last letter, and inquire about Tempie. I wanted to say a thousand things to you. That's not news, though: I always do. But never quite so intensely. You see, Mary Lou, I was and still am pretty deeply touched and terribly pleased that you would write me when you were so worried. Asthma is frightening. My eldest brother, Frank, has had it all his life, and I remember, often and often, when the spells came on, hearing him breath with that awful straining, struggling sound as though it were his last breath—the slow, labored wheezing that came through the walls from his room next to mine, where he lay inhaling fumes like the smell of burning hay from a spirit-lamp.

It made him very thin and smaller than both Bill and myself, but it didn't seem to affect his strength at all because he stroked the 150-pound crew at Yale for three years and though he still gets attacks—just had one a few weeks ago—he's quite strong otherwise.

The financial situation looks a little cheerier now. One of the letters today was from "June" Little, saying he was sending me $75 for the two rather brief articles I wrote for The Spur— about the international polo matches. Now he wants me to write some fiction for the maggy. I'll have to see what I can do.

Busy days ahead. The trial Friday, at Old Bailey, of the crack-pot who tossed a revolver at King Edward, which I'm to cover; then the Davis Cup finale at Wimbledon; possible a trip to Berlin for the Olympic Games—and it won't be long until September 15th. I haven't booked my passage yet. The final okay has still to come through from NYK. But I don't believe there will be a hitch unless a European war breaks out.

Witt Hancock hasn't arrived yet. I believe he's due now on Sunday. I'm afraid I can't meet him, though, because I've got to attend a large farewell party to Mary Sentner, Dave's wife, who is sailing back home Sunday morning at 8 A.M., and the party doesn't start until midnight! These so-long boat parties are coming thick and fast now, what with all the visiting firemen over here. They don't seem to realize, either, that we are not movie foreign correspondents, forever raising hell and high water and highballs, from dawn to dusk and vice versa, but a hard working and industrious bunch who—ourselves—look wistfully at the foreign correspondent hero as depicted on the silversheet.

And so to bed, Mary Lou. I hope for good news about Tempie in your next letter.

With all my heart,
Roge

Circa 1925

Mary Lou and Roge (center) at Princeton in 1924.

Passport photo
1924

Playing quoits with Scott Fitzgerald aboard
the S.S. *Conte Biancamano,* 1926.

Wearing chaps for a
long pack trip with
Tommy Wilder at
the Washoe Pines
Ranch, 1935.

134

1923

Roge at his desk in London
1936

London Bureau of the Asociated Press, 1936

Chapter 9

W hen they took the oxygen away, all I could think was how much I wanted it back. Please bring it back. It is so much easier to breathe. It must have tasted this way to Tempie.

Tempie.

"Tempie."

"I'm right here, Mother," she said and held my hand. "You are going to be fine."

I blinked and saw her beside my bed. I had just seen her as the little girl under the oxygen tent, and it was a jolt to look up into the face of Tempie all grown up.

All grown up, I thought, with another birthday to celebrate in a few months.

"I'm so glad to see you," I whispered.

She smiled, the same smile Roge had liked so much. I closed my eyes and tried to remember what had happened.

I was carrying a small sack of garbage out of my apartment. The next moment, I found myself on the hallway floor not knowing how I got there. I was afraid to get up fearing I might have broken a hip.

I finally decided to crawl into my apartment and dial the front desk. Then came the ambulance and paramedics and doctors and the cardiac intensive care unit. And the delicious oxygen.

It seems all my recent loss of energy was because of my heart, which finally gave up and made me black out. The doctors said I had a heart block and installed a pacemaker for one aspect of the problem. Medication will handle the rest. It is a complicated set-up for a fragile time of life.

After two weeks in the hospital, I was glad to be back in my little apartment. I had only been here a month when the black out happened, and I was surprised that it felt like home when I returned. I was glad Tempie lived nearby in Norfolk, and Mary Lou was in Bluefield, and that my daughters could come to see me.

I am up and around the apartment with help now, but it is a slow come back at my age. They say I will have more energy as soon as the medication and pacemaker work together.

I think I must get my affairs in order. I should divide up the photographs and make separate albums for the girls. I should go through my journals and decide which ones to save and for whom. I should do something about all these letters from Roge.

I wonder what has happened to him in the last sixty years and decide to send an inquiry to Alumni Records at Princeton. He was only there for that one year, but perhaps they kept up with him and will send me news. In the meantime, I rest and remember. I wonder if Roge saved my letters.

July 22, 1936

Dear honey Mary Lou:

This has been Bluefield Day—and what a thrill!

Three times . . .

But to unwind the reel in chronological order: The alarm-clock screeched at 6:30 A.M., and since Mother had stayed overnight with some friends, I cooked my breakfast kippers while I shaved and then caught the 8:20 boat-train from Waterloo station to Southampton—took the tender down the estuary to meet the S.S. Bremen and a Dr. Thomas G. Tickle, of New York. NYK had cabled us last night: "DOCTOR TG TICKLE NEWYORK ARRIVING BREMEN PERFORM OPERATION FACIAL PARALYSIS MEMBER ROYAL FAMILY." So down I went to meet him.

Coming back to London, over lunch, he mentioned that he was from West Virginia. "Not Bluefield?" I said. "Why, yes!" he said, "How do you know that?" I didn't, of course, except that West Virginia and the whole South meant Bluefield to me. So he said, yes, he knew the Archers and Hancocks, though he left there ten years ago. Well, I simply glowed! Anybody coming from Bluefield is tops—and incidentally, rather important, too, he unfroze when I told him I knew Mary Lou: you see, he's here very secretly and has been warned strictly not to talk to newspapermen and at first he denied that he was over here to treat a member of the royal family: in fact, it's so secret that he doesn't know yet which member it is, although I've an idea it is Queen Mary.

All right! Then to the office—and a thin, dark, rather shy lad came up and introduced himself as Witt Hancock. Bluefield No. 2! And then, the greatest, sweetest thing of all—your letter! My dear, it was exciting to read—pretty damn sweet and sweeter than that. Glorious! You know, Mary Lou, you are a pretty remarkable young lady. I want to remark about you all the time. I want to announce things from the housetops, and whisper things to the winds—things I have never felt before at all, things that bewilder and hurt and hearten me and make me stunningly happy, all at the same time . . .

It was an American old home day today. When I got back to the office, I cabled a piece to NYK about it—a feature yarn, starting: "IT AMERICAN OLD HOME WEEK WATERLOO STATION TODAY etc"—because after lunching with Dr. Tickle I strolled through the train and met Edsel Ford, Henry Ford jr., then bumped into Bobby Jones and Grantland Rice, with their wives, and we had a grand talk—they are both utterly charming—and the Great Grantland told me he would tell Alan Gould, sports editor of the AP, that he had met and talked with me, which will boost my stock with Alan. I was very tickled, his being so nice, and he so famous in this newspaper racket. Then leaving Waterloo station, I saw ex-mayor Jimmy Walker of New York, greeting some people arriving on the boat-train, and I stopped to talk with him a few minutes, pleased again that he remembered me from more than a year ago even though he does insist on calling me "Rogers." Maybe I seem plural to him, I don't know.

In the same mail with your letter was a copy of The Spur, with my polo article all beautifully set off with photos of Eric Pedley and Winston Guest and Mike Phipps—under my nom de plume of "Robin Densmore," because AP correspondents are not supposed to write for outside publications.

The phone—well, this is old home week, with a vengeance! It was Dr. Leo Madsen, my old golfing friend from Santa Monica, who performed the operation which brought Shirley Temple into the world—in contrast to wild-eyed yarns that Shirley is really a midget, thirty years old, and married! Wants me to take dinner with him tomorrow night. I said yes, though darn it, I meant to take Witt Hancock to dinner tomorrow. Should have taken him tonight, except that I couldn't wait to get home to answer your nicest of letters.

I'm hugely cheered that Tempie is better, and that "things are looking up" for you once more. Your happiness affects me perhaps more than you know.

Witt must have come on the same boat with your letter. I didn't realize he is such an old-timer with the AP—eight years! Lordy, I'm just a cub reporter, I guess, in this outfit when I hear about these fellows who have been with the AP seven, eight and ten years—as all of them have been, at least those sent to London.

It is miraculously splendid to read that you think I have helped at all in your seeing through the rather trying days of the past year; and if I have made you happy at all, then I am happy indeed. But you have never been "tiresome and dull," my dear: if you knew how I have loved your letters, every line, every word, you would not dare to say such a thing. Why, hell and high water, Mary Lou, I love every mood you have ever had—shining high or weary, groping at life. Because you see, life is pretty slow and dull usually; it never keeps the sustained tension and tempo of a novel—a few star-shelling high-lights here and there, but mostly routine—and now, tonight at least, I don't know but what the quiet, smooth-flowing rhythm of life is the best. I should hate to live in a drawing-room, however gay, however sparkling the company, all the time. I say all this because I am forlornly afraid that when you see me, you will be disappointed because in my letters I mostly depict only the star-shelling high-lights of my life—and believe me, honey, I am no movie "foreign correspondent" hero. If I can find any excitement, I'll take you to it; but mostly, I'm afraid, you'll find I'm just an average guy and not a character in fiction, at all, at all.

Yes, you're right—and beautifully expressed—"We are both shooting at the stars." That is very lovely . . . shooting at the stars . . . and when stars collide!!?!

I wasn't very clear, I think, about what I wrote on the matter of the beach house and all the servants. I chuckled over the picture you drew—of you all packed in the car—and loved it; and then I got to thinking: "Cars—servants—big beach house—and that's the girl you're mad enough to think you can entertain or even maybe make love you—you poor sap! Why, you haven't a ghost of a chance—she's used to every luxury and just how far do you think all your weekly pay-check worldly goods would go towards . . ." And so I wrote, "And all my dreams lie in ruins." Because I can't take you, night after night, to the expensive bright-spots. It is no use pretending. Mostly, I suppose, it can only be to grubby though perhaps amusing little spots in Greenwich Village, with wine-spilled table covers and spaghetti and crazy people and thick-blue smoke, or cheap seats at the opera, or God knows, I might even take you prowling down through the waterfront district, to the markets, heady with the fragrance of early morning and of vegetables and fruits and pine-wood boxes, and God knows, too, you might like it, though it is dark and tough and creepy until the first morning light comes dancing in against the darkness and then you love everything in what seems a sudden new world. In San Francisco, when I was collecting material for my column, I used to prowl down in the market zone around 4 A.M. and talk to the odd characters you meet then. You discover an eerie race of Night People who never see the sun, who sit on pine-wood boxes, under the fitful light of arc-lamps, and wait for the dawn that ends their day.

Anyway, Mary Lou, back-tracking to the main theme that started me on the long digression, I am so glad to read that you are "not rich! in reality, dreadfully poor." It helps a lot, because at present I simply couldn't compete.

"Handies" has finally reached England—the newspapers here have been full of them: "A Farewell to Arms," "Feeling Low," and the whole bunch. They copy every American fad, ape every idea—for example, there are now two weekly news-magazines which are dead steals on "Time" in style, make-up and everything else—but so far, in my two years in England, I have yet to hear of a single new idea originating here. They haughtily despise us for being a vibrant, young race—"quite too, too barbarous, my deah, these Americans!"—and yet they imitate everything we do.

And so to bed, Mary Lou. It's been a long day and I can scarcely blink awake. If it matters, I love you. If it doesn't, I still do . . .

More than ever,
Roge

July 24, 1936

Dearest Mary Lou:

This is, of course, getting hysterical.

My letters will be getting in your hair, and you'll be thinking, "Well, it's nice to hear from him once in a while, perhaps, but what the hell—does he think I'm a post office or something?"

And yet . . . irresistibly, even after a crowded hard-hammering day, I turn to the typewriter once more, here at home, because—I don't know why, but I suppose because my mind is so tumultuously full of you and this is one way of letting off steam. So much happens. There are so many things I want to say to you. And—oh, darn it all, you see—I've never felt this way about anyone ever before. Which is not, as Michael Arlen once said, so absurd. A few months ago, maybe, yes. But just in recent weeks you've emerged from a sort of shadowy being, a memory, into something vibrant and real and vivid. Like a dream come true. I think it was one crisp sentence that did it, when you said: "And all I know is that I want you to come back . . ." I didn't know quite what to think of the other letters. I thought maybe you had a pretty romantic bee buzzing in your bonnet and maybe thought it was sort of exciting to exchange letters with a fellow a long way away whom you vaguely recalled from a long

144

time ago. And—alarming thought!—maybe you're just stringing me along on the premise even now. If so, it will amuse you to know that I love you deeply and terribly.

I even revert to kid adverbs "deeply and terribly"—such as I dimly recall having written you as a frosh at college, and migod, here I am, ten or twelve years later, a supposedly graphic-styled foreign correspondent, supposedly with a well-developed knowledge of words, using a horrible combination like that.

But, there it is . . .

The proofs on my new pictures came up from the photo department tonight, and I'll send you some next boat—Lord help me, in your eyes! Our NYK office asked for them to be used in some promotion ballyhoo for the AP service—photos of AP foreign correspondents. They look pretty much posed, but actually the photog set up his camera while I was batting out a cable piece hot and heavy about the trial of McMahon, the twist-brain who threw a revolver at King Edward during the procession in Hyde Park last week. I had been to the courthouse, in Bow-street, all day and this photog said, "New York wants some pictures of you," and I was all hottened up with the story I was writing whirling in my head. "Shoot when you're ready," I told him, and turned back to slamming the keys again. "Now look up," he said finally. "Not quite at the camera—just off there. That's good!" And the flash-bulb flared and I forgot about it until he brought up the proofs, which look a hell of a lot more dignified that I usually look because I was in such a hurry that I didn't even take my coat off, and this way—as you will see—I look like a novelist or something and not an honest-to-God hard-working newspaperman in his shirtsleeves.

The McMahon trial yanked me out of bed at 7 A.M. after a late night entertaining a "visiting fireman" from my old beloved Santa Monica—Dr. Leo Madsen, who brought Shirley Temple into the world, and who told me, over the third bourbon highball— (please don't mention this to ANYBODY, because it is something he told me most confidentially)—that Shirley is actually almost two years older than she is supposed to be. In fact, she was born somewhere around 1926, because he told me she was one of his first patients after he came to Santa Monica, which was a year after I came there, and I drifted into Santa Monica in 1925. So

145

Shirley isn't quite so bright for her age as she is supposed to be.

Anyway, Leo and Carmine, his wife, and I went out to dinner at Gennaro's in old Soho (the Greenwich Village of London) and didn't get home until about one ayem, so I hadn't any too much sleep when the alarm cracked off to wake me for the trial. You may have read about it: I cabled over a good many hundreds of words: so I won't bore you with the details.

Tomorrow morning I'm off to Malvern, 138 miles from London, to cover the opening of George Bernard Shaw's "St. Joan" at the Malvern festival in the evening, and to interview the old crack-pot in the afternoon. I'll have to stay down there Saturday night and so, alas, I shaln't be able to get back for the farewell party to Mary Sentner, although when Mary and Dave and Joe Driscoll heard I couldn't make it, they rang up just a little while ago and pleaded with me earnestly to hop a late train and get back even if it was two or three in the morning on account of it is an all-night brannigan and Mary (she's a darling—and, lest you think of things, very tremendously happily married to Dave) said she would just sulk and not smile at anybody at all if the "old colonel" (meaning me) didn't come back to see her off. All this sounds conceited, I know; but it makes me so darn happy because there is nothing more I treasure in the world than having people like me. I am always immeasurably pleased—it is a kind of sudden, unexpected benediction—when people like me. I know it is vain as all hell; but I cannot describe the thrill of their going to that bother to say that they will miss me. I suppose, in the final analysis, it is because for so many years, with my one eye, I shunned people and was terrified of them—of coming into contact with them close enough so that they would discover that I was a "freak" with a bum eye. And it is only since 1934, when I put on this white patch, when I could face people without being embarrassed, for the first time, that I've come to realize how jolly and friendly they are. It is all so different . . .

But enough of introspectiveness. And enough of this letter. Up early tomorrow. I wish you were going with me. I have two tickets, and it's a lovely old-world spot, down in Malvern. We would have such fun. A three-hour train ride, probably a compartment by ourselves at that morning hour. Lunch at an old inn at Malvern. Then stalk G.B.S. for an interview: "Ah, come,

come, Mr. Shaw! I know you hate the trouble of interviews, but you just sit and we won't have an interview at all, we'll just gossip about this and that." I know how literary big-lights, or indeed any famous man, hates to talk for publication. He feels he's got to be as sparklingly brilliant talking as he is with laborious hours of efforts over the typewriter—and it can't be done. Then, after the interview, a ramble around the countryside, dinner, and play at 8 o'clock, probably a few more words with Shaw, I write and file my story via London, and then another night at the inn or back to London and Mary's farewell party.

With you . . .

Instead, I go alone. With you only

In my heart,

Roge

July 26, 1936

Mary Lou honey:

Just back from Malvern—the loveliest spot I have seen yet in England, Ireland or Scotland—a bright, clean, picturesque little village with age-old gateways and cathedrals, perched on the side of the steep Malvern Hills.

I went down Saturday morning—138 miles, through Oxford and Worcester and then into this quiet, beautiful valley—with the rain steaming down in torrents, then bright bursts of sun and then more torrential rain. And that's what the town looked like— so clean, so spic-and-span fresh-washed that it seemed like another world after the smudge and grime of old London.

Green-rolling hills and the valley . . . fragrant and sparkling. A cab took me from the station to the Malvern Hotel, where I was to seek out George Bernard Shaw. The prim, quince-mouthed lady manager assured me positively, rather angrily, that "Mr. Shaw will not see you. Dozens of journalists from London have been after him. He is seeing no one." So I began to talk to her. Fifteen minutes later, just when I was about to think, "Well, no dice. This is certainly the hardest bitch I have ever tackled"—and impolite or not, Mary Lou, that's what I thought: "bitch," and I think maybe you would think so too—when she said, in a gushing sort of a way, "Well Mr. Greene, if you were to write him a little

147

note—I'll see what I can do. But I won't promise anything. I'm not supposed to bother him. It's as much as my head is worth. But then—come along, I'll show you where to write it. Oh, dear, me, these dreadful newspaper people!"

And all the way down stairs, three flights below to the writing-room—this hotel being built all downwards on the steep hillside—she kept reassuring me vociferously that G.B.S. would not see me and that it was all a waste of time even writing him a note, but that, God knew, she was doing her best. So I sat down and flicked off a note to him—saying I represented "some 1400 newspapers, all told—or rather, all waiting to be told by G.B.S." And it worked. The old boy came striding into the lobby some fifteen minutes later and actually sounded more embarrassed at being interviewed than I used to be when I was a cub reporter ten years ago. Gad, I remember how I shivered and shook when I interviewed Franklin D. Roosevelt, Peggy Hopkins Joyce, Mary Garden, a Chicago gangster, Al Smith and a heap of others in those days. My teeth used to tremble. But I guess I'm case-hardened, because my heart didn't turn over once extra when he came swiveling in, with his white beard waving and his fierce shaggy eyebrows shuttling up and down, and asked: "Mr. Greene?" and I said, "Hello, Mr. Shaw. I was just about ready to send out a posse for you. Let's sit down and talk."

"I'm not giving interviews," he said, sitting down with a reluctant, rebellious air. "I've been refusing newspapermen all week. What do you want to talk about?"

"What do you like to talk about when you're being interviewed?" I said. "Art, politics, drama—"

"Hold on!" he said. "I'm not going to talk about a lot of things like that. Everything I've got to say is appearing in the Hearst papers—"

"Ah, our deadly rivals!" I said.

"On Monday," he said. "And they are paying me very handsomely. Why should I—"

"You shouldn't!" I admonished him. "It is practically hysterical of me to even imagine that you would talk for nothing in a highly commercial age like this—"

"Young man," he said severely, "what is it you want to

know? I like what you have written here," and he glanced at my note. "What do you want to talk about—and remember, I'm an old man!"

He's eighty. So I called him a liar, and we went on from there, for nearly an hour—a bright, quick and keen-witted old rapscallion—tedious only in spots. Anyway, I got enough out of him for about 600 words of cablese. An odd interview. Ordinarily, I take a few random notes—scraps of sentences to remind me of the whole context—but with G.B.S., I was afraid if I hauled out pencil and paper, he would break it off short. So I just made it a good frank-and-free conversation, all the time desperately storing away what he had said just now and afraid I wouldn't remember it, and all the time I was trying to store things away he was rushing on at a terrific pace, dropping "pearls of wit and wisdom," and it was the first time I'd ever tried that pencil-less form of interview. Now I think I'd do it always hereafter. Because a pencil and paper and someone taking down every word you say, when being interviewed, distracts and gives you pause: but this worked perfectly, and when I went downstairs to put it all down in my notebook, I was amazed at how much I remembered, word by word, whole paragraphs.

After phoning my story to London, I went up through the town and labored up the precipitous heights of the Malvern hill, which is really a mountain, about 2000 feet, and looked down on the toy villages and toy trains of the valley far below. I stood there, high above it all, utterly enraptured at the emerald beauty of the miniature country spread out below, with only the down-to-earth and rather indecent mocking "Bah-ha-ha-has" of the mountain sheep to distract my mood. You will never know, Mary Lou, how much I wanted you by my side, and how desperately I tried and almost succeeded to conjure up your face in the blue vaporous clouds that rolled around the peak. I thought: "Now I am happy—except that I want terribly to share it with Mary Lou." I looked at my watch. It was 4:55. I thought: "That means it is 11:55 A.M. in Bluefield, and I wonder what that sweet kid is doing. Oh, Mary Lou!" I think I said a silent, wordless prayer; thinking, looking across the green valley, across the opposite hills and the blue forever-reaching sky: "It isn't so far to her. Not really. You on a mountain-top, high above Malvern, England, and Mary Lou is just off there a little way on the far ridge—you can almost call her. You can, if you try hard enough, call her here to your side." And I closed my eyes and tried . . . Only the mountain and I will ever know how close I came to succeeding.

> There's green on the meadow and river;
> The lark seeks a loftier height;
> And Spring has come in with a quiver
> Of perfume and color and light.
>
> The lark's song has opened the prison
> Of winter-moods stubborn and strong;
> Yet out of my heart has arisen
> A fragment of sorrowful song . . .

That's a fragment from Heine—Friedrich Heine, the German poet who hated Germany and died in France.

A fragment from the pages and pages of notes, on all manner of things—poetry, literary star-shells, wise-cracks, world famous cafes, sayings by people—which I have kept, in an ever-fattening notebook for years.

I turned to it for that gem from Heine, and have been running through it again. And I find this, which somehow—though I cannot quite explain it—seems to apply to you and me and all we mean to each other:

> He whom a dream hath possessed treads the
> invisible marches:
> From the dust of the day's long road he leaps to
> a laughing star . . .

Or you might like this, culled from Goethe's "Apprenticeship and Travels of Wilhelm Meister":

"Through my weary life, to the last moment, this will be my only comfort: that although I cannot call myself blameless, towards thee I am free from blame."

Or this: from a dramatic criticism by Eugene Field: "He

played the King as if he were afraid somebody else would play the ace." Referring to some actor's interpretation of King Lear.

And this, by some author unknown:

> . . . the South . . . the honeysuckle . . . the hot sun . . .
> The taste of ripe persimmons and sugar-cane,
> The cloyed and waxy sweetness of magnolias,
> White cotton, blowing like a fallen cloud,
> And foxhounds belling the Virginia hills . . .

Again, this time from Judge Baldwin's famous "Flush Times":

> The Virginian is a magnanimous man. He never throws up to a Yankee the fact of his birth. He feels on the subject as a man of delicacy feels in alluding to a rope in the presence of a person, one of whose brothers 'stood upon nothing and kicked at the United States.' So far do they carry this refinement that I have known one of my countrymen, on the occasion of a Bostonian own where he was born, generously protest that he had never heard of it before!

And I like this:

> When a touch of frost creeps in the air
> And the North Wind's blaring bugles blare,
> When the long grey evenings gather down
> From the hills that shadow the walled-in town;
> When the dripping eves in a bleak refrain
> Chant the wail of a winter's rain:
> O, where is the poet left to sing
> A song of dream in the land of Spring?
> A song of dream that may compare
> To a pipe—a book—and an easy chair?

> When the wild blasts howl and the shadows flit
> Over the walls where the fire is lit,
> When the snow drifts deep and the driving rain
> Sings its song at the window-pane:

151

Then the dim world lies in the pit of night
And the grey ghosts shriek in the mad gale's flight:
O, where is the poet left to praise
The gleam and dream of the summer days?
The gleam and dream that may compare
To a pipe—a book—and an easy chair?

Well, honey it is 9:30 Sunday night. I'm going to splice the sheets for about ten solid hours sleep. And I hope that next winter, "when the wild blasts howl and the shadows flit over the walls where the fire is lit," it will be close beside you . . .

With a lot of love,
Roge

Chapter 10

We celebrated Tempie's fourth birthday that August. She was out of the woods, but continued to have bouts with asthma. We all worried about her constantly, most especially her sister Mary Lou, who was all set to begin school in September.

I had renewed a friendship with a childhood acquaintance who had become a doctor. Hampton St. Clair had recently returned to Bluefield to begin his medical practice after training at Harvard to be a surgeon. Hamp was a comfort when Tempie was ill and very good company when she was not.

The postman waved the letters from London at me when I entered the old post office. I had told him that Roge would be coming back to the states soon, so these final missives were trumpeted. The postman told me more than once how he would miss the letters. I had a queer feeling that I would miss them, too.

August 10, 1936

Mary Lou dearest:

Two grand letters from you! I feel like the cock o' the walk.

I could strut. I feel good all over. You spoil me atrociously, but—don't stop!!

Still, there isn't much time left now. Or rather, there won't be much left when you receive this—about the 18th, just exactly a month from the day I sail.

First, about that "tea date":

It will be one heluva lot more than that if the gods, Mary Lou, the AP and the Greene exchequer are at all favorable. What I would love exceedingly more than anything else, ca va sans dire, would be to greet you at the dock, quick. At this writing, plans call for mother to sail about September first to arrange about an apartment, so that it would be just you and me and no bother about anybody or anything else except us.

Do you think you could possibly swing it to be in New York at that time? Or maybe it would be better to wait until I get settled and know what it is all about—reporting to the office and finding where I'm to live, and all that—and yet, it would be a glorious moment, honey, if you could be there and wouldn't mind all the inevitable shuttling around of planting my baggage somewhere before we really started talking to each other.

Everything is still unsettled. NYK still hasn't confirmed my sailing on the 18th, but I don't think there'll be any hitch to that unless all hell, which is rapidly brewing, breaks out in Europe. And kismet-philosopher as I am, or try to be, I'm slightly boggled as to the financing of this overseas expedition. The Spur owes me $75 for my polo article, and "June" Little, the editor, wrote me saying his treasury department was a bit slow in forking over, and I wrote "June" about 12 days ago telling him for gosh's sakes to pitchfork the treasurer and get me the money here by September first. An even bigger item of necessity than that is the amount forthcoming from my dearly beloved but distressingly lackadaisical brothers in Syracuse, who are supposed to pay mother's fare home and promised to do so some eight weeks ago—but no word from them since. I dropped them an urgent note last week, attempting to impress on their cerebral tissues the fact that until I hear from them I am in a state of uncertainty and that the time is growing short. I mean, I've been saving every sixpence, or at least every other sixpence, for the last couple of months, but it takes quite an item of cash to transport two people from London to New York and without knowing definitely, so far, whether "June" and the fond brothers will come through in time, I'm a little uneasy.

"Bubble, bubble, toil and trouble . . ." Speak of the devil! Here, in the last paragraph, I'm brooding darkly about scraping together the wherewithal to get home, and the office calls to say there is a cable for me—private. My pulse pounded. "Mary Lou," I thought. And aloud: "Read it, please." It was from Paris. From my old San Francisco side-kick, Bob Low, just landed there from NYK and asking: NEED DOUGH BADLY CAN YOU SEND ANSWER INTERNEWS PARIS." Ruefully, I answered: "STRAPPED SUGGEST LONDONWARD." I hate turning him down, because he's a good friend and once loaned me some money, but—well, I wish I'd gone into business instead of becoming a perennially broke newspaperman. I can put him up here in London, but if I send him the money I've saved it will mean not getting back for another three months or more, and above all it will mean not seeing you this fall—and I have practically got to see you, that's all.

I don't know why I reel off all these ho-hum matters of the moment to you. I suppose it's because when I write you it seems that you are almost here in the room, lying on my bed facing the coal fire while I hunch over the keys, and that I am talking to you. God knows, I wish you were . . .

Tentatively, I've booked passage on one of the 10-day American Merchant liners, arriving in New York on September 28th. If possible, Mary Lou, please let me know when you can be in New York before I leave. As soon as I know definitely, I'll write or cable you what boat I'm going on and all about it.

Somehow, I'm convinced, it will all work out. I feel it deep in my bones. I've never felt so sure of anything, as that we will somehow, over every obstacle, get together this fall. It is a heaping shame, however, that Bluefield is so far away from New York. I thought it was just a whoop and a holler down the pike. Overnight and half a day—alas! that's even farther than Boston or Chicago, or I guess, about even with Chicago, which is 19 hours. My geography is sour indeed, but somehow I'd imagined—and I think most people just imagine geography—that it was just a few hours south of Washington, D.C., or maybe around Baltimore, and that it wouldn't be over three or four hours by train, at the most. Still,

I'm going to see you if I have to walk the whole distance bare-feet!

I am too utterly happy that you liked those two letters. You say, "How can a person be so sweet and say what means so much"—and that goes double for me about you. It will be nicer, of course, to talk to you in person—infinitely nicer—but there is something frank and unbending about letters which human beings, in their self-consciousness, never quite reach in the bluff of everyday conversation. I'd better warn you now, however, that I'm sometimes shockingly blunt in talk. It sometimes startles people.

Witt told me—and now you write something about it in your letter—that you play bridge. You are too good to be true. Everything you do seems to fit in with my notion of enjoying life—bridge, riding, golf, and lazing on the beach.

I don't know about this sinister doctor friend of yours, Mary Lou. He sounds pretty definitely Machiavellian to me. I mean, he's undoubtedly a grand guy but I'm glad I don't know him because I sort of hate him instinctively. I bet that deep down in his base, black heart he is a cad, a bounder, and what's more, a rapscallion. O, these doctors! Pardon me while I bare my teeth and snarl . . .

The sooner I get back to NYK, the better. It is getting in my hair. The Mary Lou-Roge rumor is now getting something fierce. The whole foreign correspondents' colony seems to have it all down pat. I mean, I was on the desk the other night—in charge of the whole office, with red-hot copy burning in from revolt-torn Spain, from the Olympic Games in Berlin, and a lot on continental European bureaus, not to mention the ticker tapes reeling off great rolls of copy from our own tight little isles of Britain. There were about ten telegraph editors and copy boys and stenogs working like fury, and the desk 'phone rang. Witt Hancock was sitting across from me—and maybe he has already told you, with lurid descriptive details, the answer to the question, "Was my face red?!!"

"Hello!" I snapped, busy as hell, trying to keep from being snowed under by an ever-mounting batch of copy.

"Rajah?" a Southern voice said. "Is this Rajah Greene?"

"Migod!" I said. "Is that—"

"Yes. It's Mary Lou."

I'm not going into details, Mary Lou. Or yes, it might amuse me—although I'm still crimson, thinking of it. Anyway, I hollered "MARY LOU! WELL, MARY LOU!" and the whole office just stopped and began to listen and I didn't give a damn although I could see them goggling at me, set back on their heels by my bellow, and anyway, I fell for it hook-line-and-sinker for about a minute and maybe it was thirty seconds which seems hours, looking back on it now with my face burning, before I decided the Southern accent sounded like mid-West in spots, and I handed over the phone to Witt and said, "Listen, is that Mary Lou?" So Witt spoke to the voice and shook his head, and—well, I was disappointed and burnt plenty. It was Lolita Martin, the wife of Johnny Martin (they come from Kansas), who just arrived from the NYK office about three days after Witt. She and Johnny were out with the mob at Joe Driscoll's, having a beer-fest or something, and they'd put Lolita (knowing I wouldn't recognize her voice) up to calling me and pretending she was you. When I finished work, at midnight, I went out and started very earnestly to wring her neck, but she said she didn't care, that she'd never heard anyone so glad to hear her voice and she'd just as soon die if I wanted to throttle her for keeps. But Lord, I'm darn near afraid to go into the office now, for fear someone will blast the air with a yowl of "MARY LOU!" and then cackle horribly, the way people do.

Since Witt and Lolita have come, life has been pretty strenuous. Bridge players in our crowd are few and far between, and when we found that they play, we started making up for lost time. Sessions ending at 6 A.M., and then to the office at 10 A.M., still mumbling, "I'll redouble!" while trying to write about the latest European crisis. Grand fun, but hard on the tissues.

And so to bed now, Mary Lou. I could certainly employ eight unbroken hours tonight.

Much love,
Roge

August 14, 1936

Dear honey Mary Lou:

This seems to be the "open season" on parties—and no sooner do you murmur "Now I lay me down to sleep" than the alarm-clock shrills hideously and a new day of waiting for nightfall and the next party is begun.

Wistfully, I believe that some day—some day, somewhere— I will get back to the halcyon time when sleep came eight hours at a stretch; but right now it is one brannigan after another. I suppose there is some reason—kid Greene going away and the farewells already booming, and the influx of that sleepless tribe called New Yorkers, including Witt and Johnny Martin and a lot of visiting firemen from Gotham Town. But there have been so many 6 A.M. parties this past week that your humblest, most devoted admirer, Mary Lou, is slowly getting gaunt. The pink flush of youth leaves my cheek. I grow wan. The quick, clear brain of yesterday stumbles on the rocks of sleeplessness— and I am beginning to think it is hell being a bachelor and no co-ordinating will to say, when the clock strikes twelve, "Lo! we go home!" Instead, night after night, I go barging around and about on brannigans that suddenly find daylight streaking the sky and smudgily entering the scene of high festivities— and the bright sun intruding on the enchanted lamps of night and reminding me, hand to brow, that the desk and typewriter await a few hours hence. It is fun. It is grand and glorious fun. But it is no way to carve out a career. Which is my terribly earnest occupation just now and has been for a long time.

Witt is a dandy. We struck it off at once. He's a grand lad, and my only sorrow is that he cannot seem to say much about you—the little details of what you are like—except that you are pretty stunning to the eye and a sweet kid if there ever was one on earth. Witt explains that he has been away for a long time from Bluefield, been down to North Ca'o-lina and so hasn't seen much of you, at all, and all he keeps saying is: "Mary Lou is sho' mighty fine. She's lovely. You gonna like her, plenty!" Well, I could have told him all that, with a lot more adjectives; but so far that's all I can get out of him. For a reporter, he's most lacking in descriptive detail. He hasn't said a thing about what you talked about when he dropped in on you there in Bluefield, although he must damn well know I am practically in a state of acute famine to know what you said—just anything you said. I guess he must know that if you just talked about the weather, I would yearn to have him say, "Well, Roge, she said: 'O, Witt, honey, look at that moon and the soft light glimmering on the water so soft, so gentle . . . and, Witt?'"

"'Yes, honey?'" I said.

"'Well, Witt, do you suppose it does the same thing in England that it does to me?'"

That's what I wanted him to report, unemotionally, as a good reporter should, as though he didn't know what it would mean—but he didn't say anything like that, at all, and I guess things never happen like that—except in dreams . . .

I passed on the item from the local newspaper to Witt and he was enormously pleased and whispered fiercely, "For——sake, don't mention this to anybody around the office." He's very shy—and, rather more than incidentally, a corking good newspaperman from what I have seen of him so far. He has a good flowing style, and what I like about him particularly—maybe because I'm the feature editor—is that he turns out a lot of good bright feature yarns, and works hard at it. I'm pretty grudging in my compliments, but I told Witt that I liked his stuff very much and liked the way he struck right out at the beginning, when everything over here is new and strange to him. Lord knows what right I have to comment on his work, because Witt has been with the AP nearly eight years to my one and a half. Still, I'm older and have about five more years of pretty diversified experience behind me, so I guess it's all right. Anyway, he's my very good friend. I only wish I knew as much about Bluefield as he does.

There is still no confirmation from NYK about my sailing on September 18th, although the Chief told me today he doesn't believe there will be any hitch and that he expects to hear from Mr. Evans, the foreign service chief, any day.

My polo yarn was published in The Spur of July—written under the pseudonym of "Robin Densmore," since technically no AP man is allowed to write for outside publication. Enclosed is a blurb about this guy "Robin"—all wrong, of course, for as you know I was never graduated from Princeton and there is no hyphen between the two names of the Herald Tribune, as any good New Yorker ought to know.

Got to skip now—out to Joe Driscoll's for supper and such. Lots of love, Mary Lou.

Ever and anon,

Roge

Our lives were set to collide, and I was anxious about it since they had been on a parallel course for so long. Part of me wanted to materialize on the dock in New York when Roge disembarked. Part of me wanted to make it all come true, to turn hopes and dreams into flesh and blood.

But mother wit is hope of a pragmatic kind, and I suspected our words were out of proportion to our lives. I wanted to see Roge; I wanted to see if we could feel these things face to face. But I did not want our first meeting to be dramatic enough to catapult us into a future we had not fully imagined. It did not seem wise to be waiting for him in New York, to be on the dock flashing Gatsby's green light towards the orgiastic future.

Monday, August 17, 1936

Dearest:

My room is in chaos. Lid-open suitcases sprawling and empty drawers gaping, and the fireplace choked with a myriad old letters (but NO blue envelopes) which I know, when I tuck them away, I'll never read again, yet invariably save until this bedouin career takes me elsewhere. As it soon will now.

Our lease expires tomorrow, so rather than put up another whole month's rent, we are evacuating—Mother is going out to Orpington, to stay at the grand country home of my boss, Mr. King, with a huge garden and orchard and swimming pool, while I'm going to bunk with one of my American newspaper confreres, Newell Rogers of International News Service, for a week and then transfer over to Frank Kelley's flat in historic old Inner Temple, beside River Thames.

Everything is now settled. NYK cabled Saturday night confirming the date of my departure. I sail the 18th, on a 10-day American Merchant Line ship. Mother sails the 8th so that she can get there a week ahead of time and find an apartment and so save the expense of a double hotel bill in New York.

I mustn't write long. It is already nearly midnight, and I've got to be up early and finish packing and move. But I simply must answer your sweet, noble letter. It is pretty hugely thrilling to think of you worrying about me—I mean, about my possibly not coming back. The odds are certainly a good 10-to-1. At least at this writing. The only joker would be a nice, fresh outbreak of a general war in Europe. That seems hardly likely tonight, although I wouldn't care to predict about war and peace in Europe for a month ahead—especially with the ugly situation in Spain and its attendant international complications—because peace on earth and goodwill toward men deteriorate very rapidly over here. One minute you have the family of nations "cooing like any suckling dove" and the next moment they are slashing earnestly at each other's throats. Our American people are wiser than they know to keep out of Europe's eternal quarrels.

Page two of your letter hits such a bounding chord in me. ("With shivers all over, yet," as Milt Gross would say) that I think I'd better not say anything right now—but just tell you about it when I see you. I mean, when you say, "I want you to feel these things you write me—and I want you to feel them after September, too—I want to do everything in my power to make them come true" . . . well, maybe and probably you just dashed them off, but they warm me to you pretty unbearably.

As if I needed it!!!

I get a great chuckle when you write: "Please turn on all that charm when you 'interview' me—not for publication, of course! because I know my knees will be shaking." Hell, honey, I bet they won't. Nobody was ever nervous with me. I guess I must have a kind face, or something, because people confide in me and absolute strangers—even in this chill-spined land of England—start talking to me and we get along fine. I don't expect you to love me because that is too much to hope for, but I know we'll get along very splendidly—and if I catch your knees shaking I will handle you rough and tough and probably just grab hold of you tight and hang on, because I have felt that way too, although it was a long time ago and you were the cause of it then. Looking back, I suppose it was funny, but then it seemed acute misery—the flurry of nerves that hit me, a very proud young frosh just beginning to feel he was a man or ought to be, when you stepped down from the train onto the red brick platform at Princeton Junction—so fresh and serenely calm and utterly exquisite: and I feeling all horribly red and grotesque and with an astonishing conviction that my legs had suddenly turned into jelly and my tongue lopped off. I will never forget the smooth-flowing calm and courtesy with which you put me at my ease and made my first college prom a weekend of drifting happy dream . . .

And for long thereafter.

I'd almost forgotten that it was Gordon McNeer who first introduced us. Fuzzily, I had an idea, somehow, that it was ol' Waltuh Hale, that lazy slow-drawlin' lad from Nashville, my best friend at college, who produced the miracle—although I remember now that Waltuh, with those slow mocking eyes of his following you around the dance-floor, asked me too many questions about you and who you were and where you came from and how long had I known you and why hadn't I brought you up long before—to have known you at all. So now at last, I find out it was Gordon—and I think I'd better write him a long letter of thanks.

O, Lord! There goes Big Ben crashing two ayem. Goodnight, my dear. Six weeks more—and then!

Love,

Roge

August 25, 1936

Dearest Mary Lou:

Just a line—to answer your sweet letters—and pop it into the mail in time to catch the *Normandie*.

Really sorry I haven't been able to write you a long, long letter this week: there is so much to say, but it has been a hectic time of moving out of our apartment and since then moving twice from one friend's apartment to another. We gave up our place, for Mother is sailing on the 11th, while I follow on the 18th, and we didn't want to pay a whole month's rent. So I've been living in a suitcase, first at Newell Rogers' flat in Dickens' House (the origin, by the way, of Charles Dickens' "Bleak House"—no longer at all bleak, modernized and charming) and then to Frank Kelley's flat in historic old Inner Temple.

I've stowed away everything, including my typewriter, in the office storeroom here—and so, since I'm a simply terrible penman, I've not written you "at home" after the office.

Everything is working out fine. I still haven't heard from my brothers, but the check for my article in The Spur arrived in the mail this morning—along with a grand letter from you. I'm so glad your mother enjoyed the polo yarn, and it is both vivid and exciting to me that you found my style "vivid and exciting." I'll have to read the yarn over again and see what I wrote. It was dashed off at white heat, against mail-boat "deadline," and I thought it would be pretty awful sort of scrappy.

I do hope you are feeling better—and better than that— by the time this reaches you. With the terrific extremes of cold and heat during the past six months it's no wonder you're ill, but please take care of yourself!

Thanks a lot, Mary Lou, for the new pictures. They're swell, and I'm so glad to have them. You look "mighty tender" and delightful—and then some!

Got to run now. I'll haul my portable typewriter out of storage and write you a long letter later, away from the hullabaloo of this office, which is pretty much of a madhouse now.

Lots of love,
Roge

Sept. 6, 1936

Dearest Mary Lou:

Gloomy Sunday . . . darkening grey skies . . . lazy-rolling thunder and flurries of rain . . . churchbells knelling mournfully, but otherwise the usually roaring-paced purlieu of Fleet-street and the office here are strangely silent.

The automatic ticker news tapes are humming, as they hum 24 hours out of the day, but there is a lull and nothing is being printed—pleasantly restful after the high-voltage rush of news of the past week: the trans-Atlantic flyers, the bloody and horrible civil war in Spain, the perennial alarums and excursions of Hitler, Mussolini, Stalin & Co.

This is my day off—after working until midnight last night—and the first quiet spell I've had in a long time in which to write you. I do hope you have been neither uneasy nor angry at the long spell since my last letter: I never saw the days, and nights, flick by so fast. This London crowd is a colony of night owls, and it has been rapidly getting no better fast these last few weeks what with a party almost ever night "just to get in training," as Frank Kelley put it, "for the final bang when we pour you on the boat."

Mother sails Wednesday, the 9th, and I follow on Friday, the 18th. Mine is an 11-day boat, stopping at Boston—and Lord, how I can use those days of grace!

I couldn't quite make out your next-to-last letter: I mean about not coming up to meet me at the boat and not coming up to New York at all. It sounded as though, in a burst of frankness, you had decided to tell me that the whole thing was too wildly romantic or fantastic and impossible and maybe we'd better just skip it. Those aren't your words, of course: just the impression I got. So anyway, we'll see . . .

I was greatly cheered Saturday, now that it is so close to the time of my going home especially, when Mr. King received a letter from Wilson Hicks, one of the "big shot" NYK executives, as follows:

"Dear King: Please express our thanks to Roger Greene for his excellent work on the latest "Our British Cousins" column. We like especially his description of the King's Life Guard. He has a marked talent for feature writing."

At the bottom of the letter, Hicks wrote: "CC Mr. Cooper"—which means that a carbon copy of his letter went to the Great White Father, Kent Cooper himself. Maybe I'll get that raise soon.

I bought a whole flock of Harris tweeds yesterday—glorious stuff, remarkably cheap. You can buy it here for about $1 a yard, or one-sixth of what you have to pay for the genuine Harris at home. I'm going to have it all made up into suits and overcoat when I get there, because my notion of English tailoring, despite its famed Savile-row, is pretty low. It may be treason, but I think Englishmen are horribly tailored with their wide-flowing lapels that look like they are ready to sprout wings and their skinny trouser legs and padded shoulders. Several of the lads in the office have had suits tailored here, and they chorus the cry, "Never again!" Personally, I'll take any little Yid tailor from the Battery to the Bronx and make Savile-row look sick. They've got the material over here, all right, particularly the tweed, but when they start to drape the male figure the result is apt to look like surgical bandages after a major operation.

Glad the pictures finally arrived, and very happy that you like them. If I looked pretty stiffly "dignified," the camera must have swallowed the wrong way. I'm mostly lamentably "pixilated," as Mr. Deeds would have it, and I guess the chances are I'll never grow up. If you expected to see me in my shirt-sleeves, with necktie twisted back around behind one ear, cigarette drooping from snarling lips, hair mussed, and battered hat tilted back on my head—well, I guess I'll have to go into the movies for you. Sometimes we look "tough," a la "Front Page" or "Gentlemen of the Press" or "Five Star Final," but only during a long siege on a big news break. Otherwise, the traditional sloppily-dressed reporter of the flickers is pretty much a thing of the past in modern newspaperdom—particularly in the foreign field, where you have to be dressed to meet anybody from Prime Minister Stanley Baldwin to the ex-Emperor Haile Selassie. When those shots were taken, I think I'd just come in from the Foreign Office, in Downing-street, and hadn't had time to take off my coat. It seems to me the only way newspapermen differ from other people is in their speech, which is perhaps inclined to be a little more brutally blunt, breezy and devil-may-care—as it tends to become through dealing, day after day, with human emotions in the raw. I sometimes wonder, if I've got a shock left in my system.

Enough for now, my dear.

My tea is nearly ready, and the sun has left the sky;
It's time to take the window to see O'Leary going by:
For every night at tea-time, and before I take my seat,
With lantern and with ladder he comes posting up the street. . .

And if I'm not mistaken, there's "O'Leary" now, in the person of Frank Kelley, coming up the street to collect me for another large evening of high festivity.

Ever with love,
Roge

Roge had jumped to conclusions. I had every intention of getting to New York by the end of the year. I had to plan for the care of my children while I was gone, and I knew Roge would be very busy when he first returned. So I had told him we should postpone our meeting for a bit. I cabled that he was all wrong about my letter and hoped it reached him in London. I sent one more letter to him there and another to the Associated Press office in New York.

The George Washington
New York
Tuesday night

Mary Lou dear:

New York! Milord, what a day and a thrill this has been. Back home—after two years. And how I love it and love it again! The blood-quickening spice in the air, the faces, the talk, the shops and cafes and bars and windows, the rushing realization of the Big Town again . . . I think I have never been so happy.

How can I tell you? First—

After eleven days of tossing on a hurricane-whipped sea, the steward blasted my sleep at 6:30 A.M. with the tidings:

"Coming in now, sir!" So . . . a hasty bath and shave, dress, and up striding on deck in time to see the Statue of Liberty, just turned 50, blue and lovely in the dim mist ahead . . . breakfast . . . pulses hammering . . . and at last warping into the pier . . . tedious customs and—no Mary Lou. Not that I really expected you. Or even hoped. Just dreams, that's all. Wistful sort of dreams, picturing you there . . . wondering if miracles happened.

They didn't.

Everything seemed so strange. The huge taxis, big as yachts, rushing like thunder; the old familiar twang of American voices and the good heart-warming sight of American faces: most of all, I think, I loved the savage snarling dispute of two taxi drivers, both trying to bear me away from the pier-shed, clamoring, shrilling, swearing, jutting pugnacious jaws in the healthy "sweet land of liberty" manner which no London cabby, in his feudal subservience, would ever dare to venture upon. Then up to the office—a huge, brisk uproarious place—where I expected to walk in as a complete stranger, lonely, new, unknown, and instead found that everybody knew me and welcomed me and said they were glad to see me because they had seen my stuff for a long time, and Mr. Kendrick, the second biggest man in the whole organization, tickled the hell out of me with his reception—the way he called up all these "big shot" writers and editors, who are way above me, hollering across desks: "Oh, Charley, come on over here and meet Roge Greene"—this to Charley Honce, who is Feature Editor, and again to the more or less famous Mark Barron, who used to write a New York daily column and is now City Editor of the AP.

It was pretty fine. After the introductions, I got my teeth right into the toil, batting out a couple of yarns for the wires, and then the chief editor said: "You better go out and see things." So I did. Rob Nevill, of the H-Trib, had just called and asked me to meet him at the Artists and Writers Club, on West 40th Street, and we had dinner and before dinner a good many Manhattans, which I've not tasted in several semesters, and it seemed everybody I ever knew in New York was there: Stanley Walker, former city editor of the H.Trib., who wrote "City Editor" and "Mrs. Astor's Horse" and I wondered if he would remember me now that he has become famous, and he not only did but came over to our table and we had a grand time: then Alva Johnston, who writes for the SatEvePost, and Ed Angley, and a raft of the NYK newspaper crowd—all immensely gay and smart-cracking and so clever it frightened me a little, because you know Englishmen are pretty dull of wit compared to the American standard of swift repartee, and I find that after two years in London it is a little like coming out of a convent and finding that the world has gone mad . . . I have got to start all over again.

They all went on to a musical comedy, but I begged off— because I was tired and a little bewildered by it all, but chiefly because I haven't written you for a long time and very suddenly, amid all the excitement, it became terribly important and imperative that I should get into communication with you again— even if it is only by this means, by typewriter, which you will not receive for many hours to come. So you can see that "I am faithful, Cynara, after my fashion . . ." I only know, Mary Lou, that it seemed far more important and desirable to slip off and write you than to go roaring around the town, and I have felt that way for a long time now.

But to go back—

Your cable to me in London, just before I left, filled me with tumultuous emotions. I immediately hit my typewriter and replied: "LC MARYLOU RYLAND 131 MONROESTREET BLUEFIELD WESTVA YOURE PRETTY SWEET THANKS FOREVER LOVE ROGE"—and then thundered at the cable-boy "Bring that back!" as he whisked it towards the wires, because I thought: "She just cabled that because she didn't want to hurt you. You've lost her—if you ever had her, which I doubt—just lately. And cables won't help. Nothing will help. Maybe when you see her . . . but don't go hoping too much."

I did go hoping too much, though. Night after night, sitting on the prom deck, lending a vague ear to the drowsy circle of conversation—blanketed figures in deck chairs, and a Vassar girl with blue laughing eyes humming in a soft husky voice of ineffable sweetness—watching the stars and wheel above the mast and thinking, almost believing, I could see you away up there—

Midnight. No more now, Mary Lou: I'm pretty weary. Mother has taken an apartment for us at No. 18 Christopher Street, in Greenwich Village. We move in Thursday. If you write, you can reach me either there or at the office, 383 Madison Avenue, Editorial Department.

Ever with love,
Roge

FRIDAY NIGHT: Oh Lord, I guess by this time you will be pretty furious at me, but—well, I thought I'd posted this, and here, amid all the furor and junk of moving, I just found it tonight in an overcoat pocket. Sorry . . .

GREENWICH VILLAGE, N.Y.
Oct. 2, 1936

Dearest Mary Lou:

Down below, in the street, a hurdy-gurdy man is playing "When the Moon Comes Over the Mountain," the night air is brisk and clean, and I am pretty darn happy about it all.

It is swell!!

The only tinge of gloom is that in a nit-witted moment I plunged the enclosed letter of several days ago into an overcoat pocket—and blissfully awaited your answer. Non compos mentis, or something like that. Are you all mad and never-speak-again? I wince when I think of what that "hot Southern blood" of yours may be doing about me—alas! And I feel worse than ever because since arriving back on the Main Stem I've had two glorious letters from you—one forwarded from London by a fast boat, and the other addressed simply but sufficiently, it seems, to me "Mr. Roger D. Greene, Associated Press, New York City."

Every night, I have meant to write you. I did write you on Tuesday—but forgot to let Uncle Sam know he had a new post-office box in my overcoat pocket. Since then has been a whirl. Meeting scores of new faces—grand lads, too. New work. Out to dinner Wednesday night with my immediate superior, Sherm Miller; then last night (Thursday) moving in to this sweet little studio apartment in the heart of "the Village" at No. 18 Christopher Street—a white, New England type place with green shutters, all spic and span, and quaint lines; and the apartment itself is a honey, small but friendly, with slanty roof and rough-plaster white walls

169

and nice maple furniture and black floors and a certain Bohemian air which can be quickly eliminated, along with the dubious fragrance of fried onions or "bubble and squeak," by merely pressing a switch which starts an air-condition fan to whirling in the ceiling. Nifty.

The office, though awesomely large and awfully noisy, is dandy: I'm terribly keen about the toil and my stories—one of which I enclose—are getting a fat play in the New York, and, I suppose, many other papers. I crashed the "Holy of Holies" this morning by getting a yarn I'd written splashed two-column front page of the New York Times, which has its own correspondents the world over and never uses an AP or any other story when it can possibly get its own comparable material. I enclose the N.Y. Daily News story I wrote about the "mysterious" Mrs. Simpson, who is King Edward's mistress in private life, as everybody in London knows.

Also enclosed—a bit of publicity for the boy Greene—is a yarn I wrote for the feature sheets, with illustration, self-explanatory.

They have been giving me a big hand around the office and it certainly warms the cockles, because I thought I'd be all forlorn and not too happy about leaving the small, intimate crowd there in London for the huge, bustling staff here in New York. But I've made more friends here in the last four days than I'd made before in the last four years—and it looks like a gay, bright winter ahead. I only wish—and wish hard—that you could be here too. Couldn't you, possibly?

Golly! Here I go, bragging around as usual about all my affairs before I come to the important thing, which is your letter—and oh, my dear, the cockles got warmer than you can possibly have any notion about when I read that my impression of the last letter I received from you in London was "all wrong"—and your terribly sweet "So forgive me, please!" when all the time, and lots of times, coming over on the boat, I have thought that it was I who ought to ask to be forgiven, please!

As it turned out, what with the rather staggering expense of moving into the apartment, paying the first and last month rent, buying dishes, linen and kitchen utensils, paying advance deposits on light and gas, hotel bills, laundry, etc. and another legion of

170

etceteras, it was provident, I guess, that you didn't come up, because all I could have done for you, I'm afraid, would have been a bus-ride and flapjacks at Child's, which is assuredly no way to treat the Belle of Bluefield at all, at all.

And so to my downy bed, Mary Lou, which is softer than any of the sheet-iron bunks I ever slept in, in England, and to thoughts awhile, in the darkness, of your own sweet self and of the momentous minute when you finally return, after a long, long time . . .

With lots of love,
Roge

I received these last two letters, mailed together, almost a month after Roge returned to New York. I was vexed with him for not writing sooner, realizing in their absence how much I depended on his letters. I was more upset with his line about "if you write." I had been writing him. Even my so-called "hot Southern blood" did not stop me from writing back.

I wondered if perhaps he did not want to see me and was fishing for an excuse. We both knew we were dating other people, and I thought that maybe the lovely Vassar girl on the boat had caught his fancy. I did not know what to expect, but I still wanted to find out and began planning a trip to New York for early November.

Greenwich Village, Oct. 9

Dearest Mary Lou:

You give me—hot-and-cold shivers!

I mean:

With a certain amount of rapid-fire palpitation of the heart, slowly blending into a soggy sinking condition like a dunked doughnut, I have been sneaking up on the "G" letter-box at the office for quite a few days now, until—as each time I turn away empty-handed—I have been conscious of head shaking and the

171

whisper going around the office: "Poor Greene! Too much meat has unhinged his reason."

Then today, on my third circuit past the mailbox, I fetched up with a start at sight of a thick envelope in familiar handwriting—and pounced. I whipped it open. I read, almost in one sweeping and bewildered glance, the first page—like radio flashes:

"Your faith should be broken in Southern gals . . . for I don't ever seem to come up to your particular kind of scratch about them . . . as for my temper, not Southern blood, getting mad and pouting, or whatever the proper song and dance is—also added in your letter today 'If I write such and such an address' . . . so admitted I am a total flop from that angle . . ."

It is hard to describe how it hit me—except that it hit me. All crumply. "Oh, God!" I thought, not, for once, blasphemous, "she's signing off. The story ends. What in the hell did I write in that last letter. She's burned crisp about something, and this is all there is about Mary Lou, there isn't any more. It's too bad. I don't blame her. Why should she bother about me? But it's too bad. It's bad. It's too bad . . . damn!!"

All this in seconds. Just one page. Phrases stabbing. "She's letting me down—there's somebody else and this is the kiss-off." That opening line: "Your faith should be broken in Southern gals—if I am to be an example!" That's what it said. And I thought, "That's the prelude to telling me she's gone and fallen for one of her own kind—somebody down there—and now I suppose I'll have to read a lot of words about how she's 'enjoyed' our correspondence and will always be my friend and if I should ever happen to drop in down there, Very Sincerely, Mary Lou."

The office was roaring in my ears, and the floor wallowing a little, and a voice dinned faintly: "Oh, Roge! Hey—hop it!" and I crushed your letter in my pocket, feeling sick, and growled at Sherm Miller on the cable-desk, "Well, what the hell now?"

"The hell now" lasted for five hours, slamming the keys about this would be frog-dictator, Colonel Francois de la Rocque, and about 1500 words on how they raided his French Social Party headquarters and all about him, trying, in the fury of writing, to forget about your still unread letter except that it kept poking my thigh every time I leaned over to look at the cable copy—and I

172

will be greatly surprised if all the papers do not come out tomorrow morning with a story about Colonel Francois de la Rocque interspersed with ejaculations such as the following:

"The summer home of the fiery leader of the Croix de Feu was the first target of the government raiders, who stormed over the threshold crying, 'Oh, Mary Lou, how could you?' The lean, hawk-nosed de la Rocque protested volubly, at first, then relapsed into shrugging silence, merely muttering: "I guess this is goodbye. Very sincerely, Mary Lou.' The haggard colonel . . ."

And the haggard Greene, at last at 7 pip emma, finally came up for air to breathe the more soothing, lovely lines of the next pages, starting with two words which mean practically heaven to me, "Dear Roge—you fascinate me too much for me to get mad at you." I hope you're playing that tune for keeps. I mean about getting mad. Skip the fascination. I couldn't fascinate a hummingbird.

Well, all this has taken a long time to explain—and Lord knows I ought to be fretting feverishly over an idea for either a novel or a three-part story I've been brooding about, called "Soft Shoulders," which might bring me some coin of the realm, which I seem to forever lack distressingly—but still and all, I did want to explain how I felt, Mary Lou, first plunged into darkest depths and then rocketed to splendid heights by your letter, which was a longer time in coming than Christmas morning after Christmas Eve when I was very young . . . and maybe you remember how you tossed and pummeled the pillow for a new niche for your head and swore you'd go to sleep, just make your mind blank this time and not think of anything, and then felt your heart beat like a slow-thumping hammer, alert, taut-nerved, fancying you heard the silver jingle of sleighbells above the rooftop, away off in the skies, and how you fell asleep, at last, to drift into dreams of mysterious, lovely things which we are both too old, I'm afraid, to remember now—except that sometimes that's the way I think about you.

Listen! When you write, "What can I expect—how can I mean anything to you really—I have no right to so much of your time—you are so busy—little time to think of me and write— your life is full of people—things happening every minute, I become more insignificant . . ." it tears me between flaring denial

173

and giddy rapture. I'm vain as hell. I surge, with outspread arms, flapping, to the tingling heights of your description of me as an important client in this terrestrial bucket-shop. But you know—and alas! I'm afraid I know, that it isn't so. It is nice to appear so, though, in your eyes, Mary Lou; but if you could see inside what I use for a brain you would know, day after day, how much you do mean to me really—how you have every right to so much of my time—how little of my life is full of people who matter—and how more and more significant you become. There is one question only I cannot answer: "What can I expect?" and it is my question.

Now this, going ahead with your sweet letter, is what I like, when you say you have come to depend on me "for so much—and the remarkably good humor you put me in." You see, I want to make you laugh and be utterly happy, because I seem to remember you laughing and I seem to remember that it sounded like enchanting music the whole world ought to hear. There is nothing, my dear, like the thrill of a lovely woman laughing. Men climb to stars to hear it, and cling there while others tear their fingers away—and it's a long drop down. I know little or nothing, or else a great deal, about women; but it seems to me that the purling sound of laughter from their throats—oh, they must be lovely, it's true—reaches into the higher spaces of delight. I suppose it is because laughter is next door to love—the whirling, unreasoning, all-engulfing thing called love. Maybe you've got it; I've got it.

I must read Vincent Sheean's "Personal History," and about the red-headed girl in Moscow. I'm way behind the times. I seem to have lost track of life, almost, over in London. Just in the last two weeks, before I left, I read John Gunther's "Inside Europe" and Walter Duranty's "I Write as I Please." There is so much to catch up on. Feverishly, during the past ten days, I've brought home armloads of the New Yorker, the SatEvePost, Collier's, Liberty, Time, all the newspapers . . .

Interruption. Dog-fight. Grim. To the death. Voices shouting: "Get him by the neck!" and "Choke him!" and "Stick lighted matches in his jaws!" and people milling around, taxis drawing up short, blocking the street, and then, in the midst of all the roaring village excitement, along comes a bus, huge, impervious to human affairs, blatting its horn to get through the

174

tangle snarl of traffic—and, darling, I've got to cut off here. I've got to tear hot into a piece about it: a piece called "Busses Never Stop" for the New Yorker.

Hastily, while the inspiration flows,

Ever, my dear, with love

Roge

Ocotber 16, 1936

Dearest Mary Lou:

I'm distraught about Tempie . . . sick over your anguish . . . your staying up all night . . . watching frantically . . . wondering why, why human beings were made so helpless . . . and wanting to help so much. You were sweet, believe me, to bother writing me at all at such at time.

I only hope, me dear, that by the time this reaches you, young Tempie will be up and lustily about. I don't know a darn thing about kids, except that my brothers, who each have two—ranging from two to five years old—both have written me from time to time saying that their youngsters went through the apparently most awful sieges and somehow, against all the odds, pulled out of it with the marvelous combative and recuperating powers which children invariably have. And yet you must be limp with worry. I understand, I think, a little of how you feel . . .

Life here is pretty sweet, but pretty furious. A faster pace, by far, than our little office in London. I feel—though Lord knows why, because I'm 32 now and a fairly full-fledged newspaperman—but anyway, I feel a strange hollow pit in my stomach when I come zooming into that huge City Room for the daily toil . . . the enormity of it . . . the knowledge that whatever I am called upon to write will be big stories in not one or even dozens of great newspapers, but in 1400 newspapers all over America. So my heart bobbles around. I think, "Well, probably, I pulled some crock yesterday and today they'll set me back on some minor yarn"—and instead, terrifyingly instead, the "big shot" editor calls clear across the burning ears of the other writers flogging away at their typewriters: "Oh, Roge, that was a swell story you wrote yesterday about . . ." and a few minutes later he

175

hands me the major yarns of the day. I wrote the Mrs. Simpson divorce action story—got a big kick out of reading it before I left the office at 11:55 P.M., splashed front page top in the New York Times—and I only started writing it at 10:05 P.M., but there it was, already out on the streets in print.

Today, I wrote more "Wallie" Simpson, Bette Davis, the whole story of the Spanish strife (insurgents, one story; Madrid government forces, another) and wound up with a "high-powered" piece of paint-splashing entitled "Jottings from an Associated Press war correspondent's note-book." What a job! The trouble is—or at least that's the bitter complaint—our war correspondents in Spain, including several very good friends of mine, are pretty horrific dullards when it comes to anything except a prosaic, straight-away news dispatch. They haven't got a molecule of literary "color" in their veins.

Here is my old side-kick, Elmer "Pete" Peterson, sitting up there right on the Spanish firing-line and writing back the ho-hummest drivel I ever saw. So somebody gets the bright idea around the office of translating it into a vivid, rippling, jerky-style "jottings from a war correspondent's notebook." I'm the sucker. I suppose tomorrow millions of people will pulsate and thrill over "Pete's" front-line adventures—as written out of thin air by R. Denise Greene, hunched over a typewriter, clutching his brow and pawing the air, inhaling cigaret after cigaret for inspiration, right here in New York.

I haven't got the copy here, but as near as I can remember, "Pete" wrote something like this:

"Twenty-five girl volunteers were among the Socialist forces killed when the insurgents entered the city."

Yeah, and that's swell, Pete, but is that all? Didn't you, for the love of Pete, see anything worth describing—didn't you, maybe, just off hand, for example, feel anything when you marched in with the insurgent forces and saw the corpses of these 25 girl volunteers? Good God, Pete, you're a fancy war correspondent, this isn't an Elks' luncheon or even the Kiwanis you're covering!

That's a small, expurgated sample of how I felt—trying to sit down and write a sparkling piece out of Elmer's story. He didn't say anything more about these 25 girls, just skipped blandly on to another paragraph about how war correspondents were learning how to avoid being "strafed" by enemy 'planes.

So anyway—

(Editor's note: "This is a great war for seeing things—if you duck fast enough!" writes Elmer W. Peterson, an Associated Press War Correspondent. And fresh from the firing-line, these crisp, graphic-styled jottings from his notebook tell a vivid story of war and its horrors in the blood-soaked land of Spain.)

by Elmer W. Peterson

VALDE DE LA REINA, Spain (by mail to Paris and New York, Oct. 15)—(AP).—Swift patter of feet . . . everybody running . . . frantically scrambling for cover—as though you could possibly tell, by some sixth sense, where to find safety with that big enemy bomber roaring down low over the village, at 150 miles an hour!

"When that baby hits—" my Fascist officer guide turns an eloquent thumb down.

I nod. "I know, but where's the safest place around here in an air raid, anyway?"

The thumb jerks up. "In the plane," he grins, white teeth flashing. "In the plane, señor, is the safes' place!"

We duck into the nearest cellar . . . dark . . . tensely silent . . . not a whisper from the hunched figures . . . waiting . . . waiting . . . arms and bodies stiff with fear . . . lips moving, without sound, shaping little fevered words of prayer in the darkness . . . then "All Clear!" . . . and the silence swerves to laughter . . .

Strolling through the shell-pitted streets . . . pock-marked walls and the little flattened bits of lead that whined like June bees a few hours ago . . . then suddenly, you stop—cold.

Slumped against the street barricade, just beyond . . . a girl . . . with a rifle still clutched in her hand . . . and a rose in her hair . . . a red rose . . . the petal fringes still showing white . . . and a black hole bored in the center . . .

Spanish senoritas . . . castanets and flashing eyes and a whirl of skirts above red-heel slippers . . . music . . . love . . . and life . . . "and a rose in her hair." Later, you learn that 25 of these girl volunteers were killed when we captured the city . . ."

Well, that's enough, Mary Lou. It isn't exactly the way I wrote it, because this is all from memory and I polished the original, but it shows you what goes out under the by-line of these "glamorous war correspondents"—and what they actually write.

Still, it's fun. I get a great kick out of it all—mixed with a few sidebars of praise. The Night Editor confided to me that already I'm the "chief color writer of the staff," which is pleasant, but darn it all, they don't pay me anything extra for it: I'm intolerably poor. Not that I ever need money or grump much about it; I'm pretty happy whatever happens, but I would like to have a nice home and a few good clothes—I brought home some swell English tweeds and other material, but can't afford to have them tailored up. And when I asked Mr. Evans, the Chief of the Foreign Service, for some more dough the other day (day before yesterday), he told me to "keep my shirt on," so God knows what to do. Kent Cooper, the "Great White Father" of the whole organization, wrote me a welcoming note which ended, "With every good wish for your success in our organization . . . etc." But that doesn't pay rent. And I'm being dispossessed from the apartment here in Greenwich Village because I refuse to borrow money to pay two months' rent in advance and after all the expense of paying Mother's fare and my fare back here and hotel bills and a thousand other things I didn't count on, I couldn't pay it all at once—so the smug-pussed landlord, a cocky young college, "hard-boiled business" type mug, handsome, exuding "success personality," got a court order to kick us out within ten days and entering judgment for an additional $30 over and above the $60 already paid in advance. I don't know where we're going to move to—maybe Forest Hills, maybe somewhere else in the Village, or maybe we will just ride around and around in one of those long, sleek, gorgeous-looking radio taxis with, I hope, the band softly playing "Carry Me Back to Ol' Virginny . . ."

Got to sign off now, Mary Lou. When you hear the time signal it will be exactly 2:03 A.M.

All the love there is,
Roge

Chapter 11

I boarded the train for New York on a crisp, autumn day. It was a long journey, and I had plenty of time for reflection and anticipation. We passed Princeton Junction towards the end, and I tried to reclaim the anticipation I felt in 1924 about a blind date with a fellow named Roger Greene.

It seemed like a lifetime ago, a time of spring. We were older and different now, having made the bumpy crossing to adulthood. And for the first time I wondered if our attraction to each other was simply the attraction of innocence and youth with all its personal excess. Maybe we were just trying to get back to Princeton and all our letters were a passionate effort in that direction.

Roge was busy with work and could not be at the station, which was just as well with me. It would have been hard to make as dramatic a debut as I had twelve years earlier.

I was familiar with New York and had no trouble making my way to the Seymour, an apartment-hotel where I usually stayed. I had plans to visit other old pals while there, but first I phoned Gordon McNeer, who was expecting to hear from me. Gordon was married and had become a surgeon and pioneer in cancer research. Roge and I were slated to come over to his place for dinner.

It was funny. Gordon had arranged our first date to the Freshman Prom, and now he was presiding over our next rendezvous.

Princeton is so clear to me even now, but my memory of that meeting in Gordon's apartment is full of holes and half-vision. I suppose he wore an eye patch, but I cannot see him with it. He had not worn one at Princeton. I suppose he looked older, too, but I still see him turned out in his best bib and tucker for the prom.

I recognized him immediately, and our first embrace after all those years and so many words was shy but long. Nervous and covering up, we talked gaily through cocktails and dinner about New York, politics, the whereabouts of old friends, books. We chattered on, and our talking tumbled short of our letters, and we both knew it.

Roge picked me up the next night to go to a live radio show, and we had terrific seats because of his press pass. We also went dancing at the Cotton Club and heard Cab Calloway's band. The Charleston was out of favor by then, and Roge confessed that he had never really learned it.

The night of the presidential election, we went to the A.P. office and listened to the returns. Roosevelt defeated Alf Landon. Standing across the newsroom, I saw Roge sitting at his desk surrounded by a swirl of smoke and colleagues. He looked up and found me, and his face lit up with a great smile to meet my anxious grin. That smile made me consider what we might have been, and I looked past him with a sense of wonder and of sadness. I knew I could not be part of his parade around the world, moving from pillar to post. I think I had known that for some time. Back in 1924, perhaps, but the intervening years of increased responsibility could not be erased.

For some reason, or no reason at all, we could not communicate face to face and the essence of our letters was lost in person. It was as though we were meant to remain on paper, in words, unattainable. We had written ourselves into each others' lives and now was the time to write each other out. The words would endure, but we could not. It was unbearably sad to let go.

And I realized toward the end of my stay, as we pounded the sidewalks of New York, that it was the illusion of those letters—

180

"the colossal vitality of [our] illusion"—that had sustained and motivated us during a lonely time in our lives. Each meeting in New York weakened the spell. Just like Gatsby, I thought, whose "...dream must have seemed so close that he could hardly fail to grasp it. He did not know that it was already behind him, somewhere back in that vast obscurity beyond the city, where the dark fields of the republic rolled on under the night."

We did not even get to say good-bye really. The last time I saw him was again at Gordon's apartment. We planned to have one more evening together on the *Queen Mary*, but he phoned and told me his mother was ill and he had to take care of her. So he spared us the great farewell, which would be easier to write than to live.

I wrote him once more, out of politeness or habit or the need for an ending. I did not really expect to hear from him, but I did one last time.

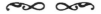

Nov. 25, 1936

Dearest Mary Lou:

The sun breaks through!

Almost for the first time since I left London, the brooding gloom that has engulfed me seems to be splitting wide-open and those "Happy Days Are Here Again!"

First of all, though, before I plunge into the nefarious details, I want to thank you for your letter. It was darned nice—and told me a lot.

I haven't answered it sooner because this seems to be a "Visiting Firemen's Week"—practically hordes of them, ranging all the way from a Bryn Mawr girl I met on the boat coming over to my lively sister-in-law, not to mention a certain amount of pre-Thanksgiving activity.

You ask for my reaction about us. Personally, however deeply and genuinely delighted I was to see you, I was wretchedly forlorn about the whole thing—so darn broke it plagued me desperately, even though you were marvelously sweet and considerate about it.

This is my second attempt at this letter . . . and it still isn't quite straight, I guess. The other was dated Nov. 23. I didn't mail it. I wanted to think about it. I'm glad I didn't. It's too high-strung dramatic, but I'll quote parts of it because it might interest you to see what I wrote first, at white-heat, in a mood of utter dispiritedness:

" . . . I didn't believe, I didn't really expect you would care much of two hoots about me: but I did dream and hope I could give you a whirlwind time . . . something you would remember, at least. But it simply didn't go off. There was a vast surplus of politeness. There was running, animated chatter. There was a lot of fun. And there was between us a wider ocean than ever separated us in Bluefield, West Va., and London, in writing. Never once was there an intimate chord struck, and out of it all, still a little bewildered, only two thoughts remain:

"1. How you ever managed to conceal your disappointment.

"2. How lovely—how forever lovely—you looked curled up on Gordon's divan, with your legs tucked under that stunning silver-edged black gown.

"There is so much to say. So many tangled thoughts. They've been drumming through what I use for a brain ever since. It is hard to reconcile things. I mean, your cables and mine. The tingling atmosphere of Before New York. The excitement! The happiness! And then, out of it all, we emerge—shall we say good friends? Good friends—and you're certainly a great, sweet kid, Mary Lou; and mine is the fault, but—good friends without much more than the ghost of a drop of the romance which was distilled and double-distilled in all our letters. Somehow I fumbled it and we talked inanities, always at arm's length. And finally, to straighten things out where I guess they belong—the saga of Mary Lou and Roge is ended."

That's what I wrote, Mary Lou, two days ago.

Gone with the wind . . .

So anyway, I was going to tell you about brighter times in the career-line. The day after Kendrick got back—after I'd thrashed out things with Mr. Evans, back from Chicago and had told him I thought he had given me a darn dirty deal and that unless he gave me a raise I was leaving the AP: and he definitely assured me of a raise and explained that maybe he'd acted a little hastily but that he did it "because I don't want to lose my job, Greene" in a snivel-lipped voice—anyway, Marion Kendrick, who is executive chief of the whole AP and next only to Kent Cooper himself, called me over and said he had heard about my deal from Evans and that he wanted me to work for him, in the American news sector, at a fine raise in salary. Would I accept? Would I! You may remember I spoke to you about going to Kendrick and of trying him before I quit the AP—well, it was a great thrill, believe me, when he came to me and asked me to work for him instead of my going to him and asking to be transferred. So that's fixed.

I started today. And it looks like I'm pretty well set, Mary Lou. They all gave me a pretty glowing reception over there on the City Desk, and although it seems strange not to write about Reichsfurhrer Adolf Hitler and Premier Benito Mussolini and Dictator Dr. Kurt von Schuschnigg of Austria and Prime Minister Stanley Baldwin, etc., ad infinitum Europa, I guess it is nice to write about American news once again.

Now: your letter. I was sorry, too, in a way, over missing our date to see the "Queen Mary." I called the hotel, got your forwarding telephone number, called it, and a soft sleepy Southern voice (this was Monday afternoon) said you would be back about 5 o'clock. I called then, got no answer. Call again, ditto. Called Tuesday and learned you had left town.

In another way, it was better as it happened, because I only had $2.17 to my worldly name and I guess I've got a complex about being broke. I was glad you had gone . . .

Have to finish this letter later. Sorry; more again. All the best, Mary Lou,

Roge

Chapter 12

S pring returned again, and my energy was renewed just as the doctors had promised. The flowers were up and so was I. I decided to stage a return to Charlottesville where I still keep an apartment.

My driver was ready, and I picked up my mail on the way to the car. It was good to be on the move again. Travel is still my thrill, even when the road is familiar and the destination well-known.

I settled in for the drive and flipped through the mail. At the bottom of the stack was an envelope from Princeton University, Alumni Records. Enclosed was the entire "public record" of Roger Greene, '27.

THE CLASS OF 1927
ROGER DENISE GREENE
(ROGE)

Greene was born May 6, 1904, in Cleveland, Ohio, and has also lived in Seattle, Wash., Denver, Colo., Andover, Mass., Los Angeles, Cal., Chicago., and Santa Monica, Cal.

He is the son of Frank C. Greene and Ruth Mary Irvine. His father is a coal geologist and affiliated with Old Ben Coal Corporation of Chicago. He has two brothers. Among his relatives is W.M.H. Greene, '26.

He prepared at Andover, where he was a member of the Class Football and Track Teams, Editor-in-Chief of Newspaper, Art Editor of Magazine.

At Princeton he was a member of the Second Freshman Crew.

Freshman year he roomed at 66 Nassau St., with W.M.H. Greene, '26.

Greene left college in June 1924 to engage in the advertising business, and is at present a police reporter.

He is an Agnostic and Republican.

His permanent address is 316 25th St., Santa Monica, Cal.

July 7, 1944

Our classmate, Roger Greene, distinguished Associated Press correspondent, accompanied the first invasion wave to reach France. With a sixty-pound pack on his back and armed with a typewriter, he waded ashore and thanks to a couple of four-leaf clovers, was able to give the hungry American public first hand news. A number of men close at hand were killed or wounded, including his escorting officer, but Roger's luck was with him on June 6. We are sure that our classmates have enjoyed his vivid stories. Thanks to his Princeton training, in spite of shot and shell there was never a split infinitive.

1947

ROGER DENISE GREENE

HOME: 1615 No. Springwood Dr., Silver Spring, Md.

BUSINESS: Associated Press, 330 Star Bldg., Washington, D.C.

NEWS EDITOR

Until 1930, Roge was columnist and sports editor of the "Evening Outlook" in Santa Monica, Calif. He left Princeton in 1924, intending to take up advertising, but succumbed to the journalistic bent he showed in prep school. From Santa Monica he went to N.Y. for a year as a staff writer on the "Herald Tribune." He wrote short stories for the pulp magazines, "scribbled" for the movies, did some ghost writing, and by 1933 had settled down to writing in Whittier, Calif. Later, he joined the Associated Press office in N.Y., and has been with A.P. ever since, turning out articles—"thousands." In the war he was overseas for eighteen months, directed A.P. correspondents on the British-Canadian front in Europe, covered the D-Day Normandy invasion, and accompanied our forces through France, Belgium, and Holland and into Germany. The War and Navy Depts. conferred upon him their certificates of merit and commendation.

He missed a lot of golf games, fishing, and gardening—and his wife, the former Eleanor Marsh Willson, married in N.Y.C., June 16, 1938, She is a fashion artist, trained at Carnegie Tech.

Roge has a Princetonian brother, Melville H. Greene '26.

35th YEARBOOK
ROGER DENISE GREENE
    HOME: Ozono, Florida, P.O. Box 116
    RETIRED: Formerly journalist
    MARRIED: Eleanor Marsh Willson (Carnegie Tech College)
June 16, 1938

At his retirement (Dec. 16, 1960) at 56 ("and damn glad of it," he writes) Roge was a feature editor for the Associated Press Bureau in Washington, D.C. He is having a grand time, golfing, fishing in the Gulf of Mexico, gardening, and taking pride in his wife's 17-handicap golf game "on a rough, tough course." He is a member of the Dunedin Country Club at Dunedin, Fla. As an "anti-Communist Republican" he occasionally heckles the governing powers.

Until he joined the A.P., Roge had a roving and interesting career, with some hard knocks during the Depression years. He was columnist and sports editor for the Santa Monica, Calif., "Evening Outlook," before 1930; staff writer, New York "Herald Tribune" (1930-31); San Francisco "Call-Bulletin" (1933-34); Universal Service (1934); plus writing for the movies, short stories for pulp magazines, and some ghosting. He was with the A.P. twenty-six years, in London, New York, Miami and Washington, writing about 10,000 news stories for their wires. In World War II he was overseas for 18 months, covering London and the war fronts. He was the first sea-borne correspondent ashore in the Normandy invasion, June 6, 1944, and for nine months covered the British and Canadian armies, as chief of A.P. correspondents on the British-Canadian front, through France, Belgium, Holland and Germany. The War and Navy Departments awarded him certificates of merit and commendation; and by order of King George VI, he was "mentioned in a dispatch, placed on record 12 August 1946," for his service with the British armies. It looks to us like a richly earned rest, Roge!

PRINCETON ALUMNI WEEKLY
5/12/64

"After 35 years of high-tension batting my brains out on a typewriter," Roge Greene retired to Ozono, Fla., not long ago. His gout having all but disappeared in the tepid Florida climate, he now plays golf almost every day at Dunedin Country Club. Roge wrote amusingly of retired life in a letter to Mitch Posey, Secretary of the Class of 1923 at Andover, which appeared in that school's Bulletin, and could not be reprinted in toto here. He gives thanks that he had the sense to retire when he still has his health and urges all classmates to do likewise. After 26 years of meeting deadline for the AP, Roge deserved to write "30" to his newspaper career.

PRINCETON ALUMNI WEEKLY
7/1/75
ROGER DENISE GREENE '27

Death took Roge from us on May 9th in a hospital in Clearwater, Fla. He is survived by his widow, Eleanor Willson Greene, whom he married in '38. Roge came to Princeton from Andover, where he was editor of the newspaper, but he stayed in college for only one year, leaving to engage in advertising.

Roge had an interesting life. He became a police reporter, then sports editor for a paper in Santa Monica, Calif., then a staffer for the "Herald Tribune" and later for the San Francisco "Call-Bulletin." He wrote for the movies, for the pulp magazines, and did some "ghosting" on the side. In '35 he joined the Associate Press and was with them for 26 years, in London, New York, Miami and Washington, writing some 10,000 news stories.

During World War II Roge was AP war editor in N.Y. from May '40, when Hitler invaded the Low Countries, to the fall of

'43 when he went to London. He stayed overseas for 18 months, landing with British troops on D-Day, the first sea-borne newsman ashore. He directed correspondents on the British-Canadian front, and later accompanied our forces through France, Holland and Germany. He received certificates of merit and commendation from both the War and Navy Depts., and by order of King George VI was "mentioned in a dispatch and placed on record 12 August 1946" for his service with the British armies.

Roge retired at the end of 1960 and had lived in Ozona, Fla., ever since. We send our sympathy to his widow in her bereavement.

The Class of 1927

I read the records several times before I realized I was not stunned by his obituary. Somehow I knew he had already died. Like Gatsby's father, I have reached the "age where death no longer has the quality of ghastly surprise." I have outlived so many people—parents, brother, husband, and good, good friends—it was not unusual for me to expect news of Roge's passing.

Princeton confirmed my guess, and I let myself wonder what I would have done if the news had been different. I could have called him, and I smiled as my imagination filled in the conversation.

"Roge," I say, with an increased Southern accent. "It's Mary Lou."

"Mary Lou?" he booms back. "Why, Mary Lou, is it really you?"

"Yes, Roge. How are you?"

"I am well, but somewhat speechless at this exact moment."

"I'm sure you can think of something," I tease. "You were always marvelous with words."

"Yes, and I borrow words when at a loss," he laughs. "How about some Fitzgerald: 'Boats against the current, borne back ceaselessly into the past'?"

"I've read that before and thought of it often," I say softly.

"I read that they put those words on his gravestone, you know."

"Roge?"

"Yes?"

"I have all these letters, and I've been thinking about you."

"Those letters," he chuckles. "There were quite a few of them, I think."

"Yes, quite a handful from my dashing foreign correspondent," I say.

"I have a stack of blue envelopes squirreled away somewhere. Or at least I used to. Those lovely blue envelopes with the familiar handwriting," he says, trailing off.

There would be a pause and then we would dive into the events of each others' lives. He had married Eleanor Willson in 1938, accompanied the British forces on D-Day in Normandy, and gone on to have an extraordinary career with the Associated Press. I wonder if his wife was the girl he had met on the boat when he returned from England. Many shipboard romances arrived at the altar back then.

I tell him that I married Hampton St. Clair, that doctor friend of mine, in September of 1937 and had two more beautiful daughters. He is amazed that I settled in Bluefield, but glad to hear that we managed to travel a bit when the girls were older and travel a lot after we retired to Charlottesville in 1968.

"Roge, what should I do with all these letters?"

"Pardon me?" my driver asks, and I realize I have left my silent conversation and asked this question out loud.

"Oh, nothing," I say to my driver and look out the window.

"We're almost to Charlottesville now, aren't we?" I ask like the anxious child on a long journey.

"Not too much longer," he says, sounding almost parental.

Chapter 13

I settle into my old apartment quickly and have a light supper. Tempie calls to make sure I am all right, and I tell her about the envelope from Princeton, which I have placed on top of the box containing Roge's letters. She is glad I have determined what became of Roger Greene.

I turn on the television and sit down on the chaise with some forgotten needlepoint, but my mind wanders. All my questions about Roge have been answered, but I am unable to close the book on him. Just as I was always unable to throw away his letters.

If we could have had our conversation, I wonder what he would have advised me about the disposition of these letters. Would he have wanted them returned or burned? And would I have wanted mine tossed on the ash heap, too?

His letters were a gift that could not be returned or discarded. We had written to each other during a lonely interlude, when the facts of our lives seemed like fiction and the mundane was pierced by numberless dreams.

There is room for wonder in every life, and in that room we find the unattainable that fuels our dreams. In that room, I keep Roge's letters and in those letters I find the book he had hoped to write.

The television interrupts my resolution, and I notice the program is anticipating tomorrow's fiftieth anniversary of the D-

Day invasion. I had not known until this day that Roge had been a part of it, and I watch the old newsreels wondering if I might catch a glimpse of him.

I sleep late the next morning and after foraging for breakfast, call the grocer who will deliver food and the local newspaper. I watch more of the D-Day ceremonies and begin pulling Roge's letters from the envelopes and stacking them in order for photocopying later.

The delivery boy arrives with my groceries. I put them away and then sit down to read the paper. There is an insert commemorating D-Day. I pull it out, turn to the first page, and am glad to be sitting down.

Two articles by Roger Greene are before me. I read them and recognize him in each line. They sound just like Roge.

ASSAULT INTO FRANCE MOVES AHEAD QUICKLY
Correspondent reports from the front lines
by Roger Greene
ON A BEACHHEAD IN FRANCE, June 6, 1944 (AP)—Hitler's Atlantic wall cracked in the first hour under tempestuous Allied assault.

As I write, deeply dug into a beachhead of Northwestern France, German prisoners, mostly wounded are streaming back. But the Boche still is putting up a terrific fight.

Shells are exploding all over the beach and out at sea as wave after wave of Allied ships, as far as I can see, move into shore.

My escorting officer, Sir Charles Birkin, was slightly wounded three times in the first 15 minutes ashore and three men were killed within five feet of me.

Our heavy stuff is now rolling ashore and we not only have a solid grip on the beachhead but are thrusting deep inland.

The beach is jammed with troops and bulldozers for many miles, and now it has been quiet for 15 minutes, which apparently means the German big guns are knocked out.

Our casualities on this sector have been comparatively light.

I landed at 8:45 a.m. wading ashore waist deep in water under fire to find quite a few wounded and some killed on the beach— and Nazi prisoners, very stiff and sour-looking already coming back.

Before embarking we were told there would be 10,000 Allied planes attacking today and there is every sign our air mastery is complete. So far not a single German plane has been seen.

German prisoners said Hitler visited this beach two days ago and they admitted that they were taken by surprise.

Only a few hundred Nazis manned the beach defenses on this sector. They laid down a terrific machine-gun fire, but were quickly overwhelmed.

As far as I have seen there is no sign of Hitler's vaunted Atlantic Wall with its massive concrete fortifications. German artillery deeper inland is very formidable, but the beach defenses are piddling, rifle-slits and strands of barbed wire.

"ATLANTIC WALL" NOT TO BE FOUND
German defenses not as strong as claimed
by Roger Greene
WITH THE ALLIES IN FRANCE, JUNE 6, 1944 (AP)—As far as we could see after advancing five miles inland, Hitler's vaunted "Atlantic Wall" is a myth. The thickest barrier I have seen is a crumbling old brick wall, two feet thick, along an apple orchard where I am sitting deep in the grass writing this story.

The crackle of rifle fire some 500 yards away is intense, and every few minutes we throw ourselves flat and try to squeeze our whole bodies under our battle helmets as German shells burst in the orchard nearby.

Aside from scattered pillboxes, barbed wire and silt trenches, the German static defenses so far have been practically nil, and in this sector at least we have seen nothing of the great concrete fortifications 12 feet thick which the Germans had boasted they had erected along this coast.

Their mobile artillery appears their most formidable defense, and while their planes are fairly much in evidence they are only specks in the sky compared with the great clouds of Allied bombers and fighters which sweep over our heads in endless waves.

German death's head signs of "Minen" (mines) are frequent along the roads, but there is no evidence of the "millions" of mines which the Germans said they planted.

We walk along with extreme care, however, along the center

of the road, or along truck tracks where the way has been cleared.

This has been a tremendous day. I crossed the channel in a small, heavily rolling LCI (landing craft infantry) with 100 men. It was a rough crossing, but without attack by German U-boats, E-boats or planes.

Although I believe I was the first correspondent ashore, I had to wait more than five hours before I could send my first story back by boat.

The press field radio which was scheduled to arrive early on D-day still has not shown up.

The first Frenchman I met after landing said the Allied naval and air assault preceding the landings shook the whole countryside like an earthquake.

"Alas," he said, "we had wine saved to greet the Allies, but now it is gone. Pouf—bombs and wine do not mix. Veree sad."

I am happy to the point of tears and read them again. On the television, old soldiers who had survived and old journalists who had been there are interviewed as they walk on the beach and around the cemetery. I shut off the television and realize I am glad I did not know Roge as an old man but as a young freshman with whom I sipped early morning milk while watching the sun dawn on our horizon of dreams.

October 12, 1926

Dear glorious Mary Lou—

Are you divine? Or why does the sight of your quaintly adorable handwriting send me into a thousand ecstasies?

Ha! An absurd question, because I already know the answer and it is this. It is the faint-intoxicating outline of Mary Lou in a box at some moving picture in New York which I never saw— nor learned its name. A rather drab and unromantic spot for a romance to start—the box in a New York cinematograph.

As I watched you there—very impolitely, I'm afraid—I felt, I

194

don't know why, as though my heart had once been broken.

Now I think it will never heal, unless—but that is a mad fantasy.

I'm happy to know you liked that "High o'er the hill the moon barque steers. The lantern lights depart." It is from "The Lute of Jade"—a collection of Chinese poets edited by L. Cranmer-Byng.

There are many beautiful songs in "The Lute" and it is a splendid volume to have in your library.

Here is another. I've forgotten by whom it was written—that I find in my notebooks.

> Across the fields of yesterday
> He sometimes comes to me,
> A little lad just back from play—
> The lad I used to be.

> And yet he smiles so wistfully
> Once he has crept within,
> I wonder if he hopes to see
> The man I might have been.

It was a chill, wet day here today—rain all morning, but it stopped this afternoon and Bill and I went out for 18 holes of golf. The fairways were a bit heavy and a cold wind whipped in from the ocean, but it was heaps of fun and over every hilltop—very brave and beautiful and trim-looking—I felt was Mary Lou—just beyond— almost within reach—almost tangible. I blundered my shots badly— looked up to see if you really weren't there.

And then at sunset—coming up the 18th hole facing the Pacific— and a marvelous sunset . . . the fire-shot clouds, bursting with scarlet color—it seemed quite too beautiful for the moment—then suddenly the sun falling away and the clouds hanging leaden and grey like some burnt out bit of powder. The transition is tremendous . . . inconceivably brilliant with colors baffling description—then, as though all life had been driven out—the sunset gone and the clouds mottled, dull, sombre with the approach of night.

You must read "Soundings," Mary Lou. Because the girl, as I read it through, was just Mary Lou under another name. And I fell desperately in love with her. The book is by A. Hamilton Gibbs and is listed in Brentano's as one of the six best sellers.

About my story, Mary Lou. The more I consider it, the deeper I am convinced that I must get away—travel and all that before I can write. It is—I think I can say without boasting—fair in some spots, but decidedly murky in others.

Won't you be satisfied if I promise to send you my first M.S. which I think is at all decent? It shall, I hope, be soon.

Holton Arms must be splendid. I don't remember Elizabeth Scudder—but, can you blame me? I could only think—and that in a rather heart-pounding fog—of Mary Lou that night.

It seems such a short time ago since the Proms—Gods! how the months fly by. I dread the day when I will open a letter from Mary Lou—I, a doddering old gentleman sitting in an armchair before the fire—a bachelor—and learn that the years have galloped by with startling rapidity. (I hope we will still be writing by that time.) Do you remember Robert Louis Stevenson's "Windy Nights"?

Whenever the moon and stars are set,
Whenever the wind is high,
All night long in the dark and wet,
A man goes riding by.
Late in the night when the fires are out.
Why does he gallop and gallop about?

Mary Lou dearest—I love you for thinking about me, but— since I'm profoundly vain—do you like me a little bit? Ha! I should not have asked that. But I am so hopelessly mad that perhaps you won't mind.

There is a comic side to my writing you, for while I am not afraid to tell you how sincerely I like, love, adore—dammit, the English language is peculiarly cold and inexpressive—you from my desk in California and you in the East—were I to see you tomorrow, I should be dreadfully shy and awkward and would probably be telling you how glad I was to see you and talk about the weather or prohibition instead of expressing an inexpressible, maddening desire to hold you very tight forever.

Please forgive me. Ever with love,

Roge

316-25th St.
Santa Monica, California

196

Mary Archer St. Clair was born in Bluefield, West Virginia. She is a graduate of the Oakhurst Collegiate School attended Holton Arms Junior College. She also studied in France at the Finch School's program in Versailles. An enthusiastic traveller, reader, and artist, she now lives in Charlottesville, Virginia.